Volume 4

Bulgaria in Europe

Series Editors

Dimitris Keridis

Charles M. Perry

T0339102

Potomac Books, Inc.

(Editorial)   22841 Quicksilver Dr., Dulles, VA 20166 USA

(Orders)   Potomac Books Orders, P.O. Box 960, Herndon, Virginia USA 22070

Library of Congress Cataloging-in-Publication Data

Bulgaria in europe

ISBN: 1-57488-955-9; $28.00

CIP information not ready at time of publication

Designed by J. Christian Hoffman

Printed in the United States of America by Daniels a Merrill Communications Company, Everett, Massachusetts

10 9 8 7 6 5 4 3 2 1

Bulgaria in Europe
Charting a Path Toward Reform and Integration

Editors
Dimitris Keridis
Charles M. Perry
Monica R. P. d'Assunção Carlos

A Publication by

The Institute for Foreign Policy Analysis, Inc.
In Association with The Fletcher School, Tufts University

The Kokkalis Program on Southeastern and East-Central Europe,
John F. Kennedy School of Government, Harvard University

The Kokkalis Foundation of Athens, Greece

Potomac Books, Inc.

Contents

Part 3. Bulgaria in a New Southeastern Europe: Priorities and Challenges Ahead

Contents

1 Introduction

Dimitris Keridis and Monica R. P. d'Assunção Carlos

Bulgaria in Europe is an assessment of Bulgaria's progress toward fulfilling the economic and political criteria for accession to the European Union (EU) and the North Atlantic Treaty Organization (NATO). The point of departure for this volume was the conference "Bulgaria in Europe," a meeting organized by the Kokkalis Program on South-East and East-Central Europe at Harvard University's John F. Kennedy School of Government and by the Kokkalis Foundation of Athens, Greece. The meeting was held on July 15, 2002, in Sofia, Bulgaria, just five months before NATO's Prague Summit, where Bulgaria was invited to join NATO. Bulgaria stood on the threshold of the new millennium, with several challenges looming on the horizon, and the conference aimed to explore the country's geopolitical environment and its international and domestic strategic agenda in relation to EU and NATO enlargement.

Along with the proceedings of the conference itself, this volume includes a select group of studies contributed by invited officials and experts. Over two years were necessary to put together this collection of studies because of the time-consuming and often painstaking work of gathering and using data on a country with limited and underdeveloped research sources. By publishing the conference proceedings we hope to bring the discussions and conclusions that were reached in this meeting to a larger audience at a critical point in Bulgaria's development. The research contributions complement the views presented at the meeting and together with the proceedings make up a volume that offers an overall evaluation of the country's transition efforts and developmental challenges – as they stood in mid-2002 – by identifying areas of improved policy performance and probing areas of continued, or new, policy underperformance. Where possible and appropriate, the volume's editors have updated the contributions gathered here to reflect changes and developments since the individual pieces were completed.

Both timely and important, the meeting was a unique endeavor that brought together representatives from politics, media, academia, and the private sector with diverse areas of expertise with the purpose of assessing the progress Bulgaria had made in fulfilling the economic and political criteria for EU and NATO accession, and to examine the country's short- and medium-term foreign policy strategies. The group of participants gathered was of impressive quality, including as it did senior government officials, representatives from Euro-Atlantic institutions, affiliates of international organizations, and leading experts from the academic and policy communities on both sides of the Atlantic. The conference panels were designed to address three different but interrelated subjects: Bulgaria's current foreign policy environment; the progress of economic reform; and issues of democracy, human rights, and domestic institutional reforms.

The clear, overall consensus that readily emerged at the conference was that Bulgaria had come a long way and had made considerable progress in consolidating and deepening the stability of its institutions, thus guaranteeing democracy, the rule of law, human rights, and respect for and protection of the rights and freedoms of all ethnic and religious minorities. Most importantly, the transition years were rich in reform breakthroughs without any major setbacks and without any incidents of violent conflict. Regarding economic reforms, the Bulgarian economy was going into its sixth year of stability, having established a satisfactory track record of macroeconomic performance, which makes for tremendous progress toward convergence with the European family of nations[1]. The old "laggard" of the East European transitions lagged no more. From an annual growth rate of minus 10.1 percent in 1996, its GDP growth in 2000 increased to 5.8 percent. Investment grew by 8 percent and contributed, together with net exports, most to aggregate demand. Manufacturing expanded most rapidly (by 15 percent), while services expanded at half that rate. Inflation decreased from 121 percent in 1996 to 10 percent in 2000. At the end of 2000 unemployment had fallen to 16.4 percent of the labor force.

Since the 2002 conference, progress toward integration has been fast and steady. Bulgaria joined NATO in April of 2004 and will sign the EU's accession treaty in April 2005. These historical developments are the culmination of Bulgaria's efforts and improved performance. Buoyed by a rate of global economic growth expected to reach 5 percent in 2004, Bulgarian real GDP grew by 5.8 percent year on year in the third quarter of 2004. Growth in 2003 was 4.3 percent, which was the fourth year in a row in which real growth exceeded 4 percent. Third-quarter growth was sustained by an acceleration of spending on fixed investment, and by the fact that exports rose more quickly than imports. Gross fixed capital formation grew by 14 percent in 2003, and it represented 19.5 percent of GDP. The industrial component of total gross value added increased by 5.1 percent year on year in the third quarter of 2004, and the services portion increased by 5.9 percent. Inflation has been on a downward path, from an average annual rate of 5.8 percent in 2002 to 2.3 percent in 2003, mainly because of low food prices and low import prices following the depreciation of the dollar. However, increases in food and petrol prices as well as an increase in excise duties brought

---

1 The data reported in this section are drawn from the Regular Reports on Bulgaria's progress toward accession, published by the European Commission's Directorate for Enlargement.

inflation to a peak of 7.6 percent in July 2004, according to the estimate of the Economist Intelligence Unit, or EIU (2005).[2] In its 2002 Regular Report on Bulgaria's progress toward accession, the European Commission found that Bulgaria made reasonable progress in privatization, especially with regard to banks and structural reform, thus setting the microeconomic basis for sustained growth. Despite the new legal framework for privatization put in place in April 2002 to provide clearer rules and greater transparency, privatization advanced more slowly than was hoped because of procedural problems and moderate interest by foreign investors, the latter also due to the weak state of the global economy. Further, a major reform of health and pension systems is underway. Bulgaria is close to being a functioning market economy and it should be able to cope with competitive pressure and market forces within the European Union in the medium term, provided that it continues implementing reform and intensifies the effort to remove persistent difficulties. In fact, since 2002 the European Commission has recognized that Bulgaria has a functioning market economy.

The 2003 Regular Report on Bulgaria's progress toward accession identified as the country's main challenge the ability to strengthen the capacity of, and coordination between, the various bodies responsible for intellectual and industrial property rights protection, so that these rights are enforced in an accurate, timely, and transparent way, thus increasing business confidence. Bulgaria needs to persist in and intensify its efforts to develop a more favorable business environment, and to address the administrative, financial, fiscal, and managerial obstacles to the creation and development of small and medium-size enterprises (SMEs). Private investment remains insufficient and needs to be promoted more vigorously. Bulgaria has already begun the process of removing and streamlining numerous licensing procedures, and it has taken measures to reform its judicial system in an effort to improve the business environment. Foreign direct investment (FDI) net inflows increased from $109 million in 1996 to $806 million only three years later, with gross capital formation jumping from 8.4 percent of GDP to 19 percent of GDP in those same years. Net inflows of FDI of 3.9 percent of GDP in 2002, after 2.6 percent in 2001, were again lower than the current account deficit, although in 2003 FDI inflows increased by 56 percent, from $900 million to over $1.4 billion. More than half of total FDI is channeled into industry; trade, finance, and tourism are the next most important sectors.

As elsewhere in the region, growth in Bulgaria has slowed recently, in part because of the impact of the external environment, in part because of government underperformance. The conference participants stressed the need for Bulgaria to catch up with the more advanced transition countries as much as with the European Union itself, and identified three major clusters where domestic political reforms must be given priority: public administration and the protection of minorities; education

---

2   The EIU (2005) forecasts a 3.7 percent inflation rate for 2006.

policies; and unemployment and labor market flexibility. Politically, the policy priorities are control of corruption and reform of public administration and the judicial system. Even though Bulgaria has adopted an action plan for judicial reforms and has approved major amendments to the Law on the Judicial System, these now need to be implemented with concrete improvements that have a tangible impact in the judicial process. Similar implementation efforts are needed with regard to the action plan for the modernization of the state administration and the Bulgarian national anticorruption strategy, which will ensure an efficient, transparent, and accountable public administration. Bulgaria also needs to take further measures to ensure the full protection of human rights and freedoms. Some participants addressed the issue of protection of ethic minorities such as the Roma community, and it is also imperative to fight social discrimination and the deterioration of living conditions for those living in state institutions for the handicapped and childcare institutions. Overcrowding and poor services continue to be cause for serious concern.

The employment rate of the working-age population was slightly up but was still low at only 50.6 percent in 2002; in the third quarter of 2004 it fell to 45.3 percent. The unemployment rate decreased from 18.1 percent in 2002 to 11.0 percent by the third quarter of 2004; the estimate for 2006 is on the order of 10.5 percent (EIU 2005). Over 60 percent of all unemployed are long-term unemployed. Unemployment for persons between fifteen and twenty-four years of age was 24.9 percent in the third quarter of 2004, and regional patterns are pronounced. While at the end of 2002 the unemployment rate was 11.8 percent in the southwest region (which includes Sofia), it was above 15 percent in all other regions, reaching 22.8 percent in the northwest. Bulgaria needs to focus its efforts on the implementation of antidiscrimination and equal opportunities in the labor market.[3] Further labor policy efforts are also critical for added flexibility and to reduce non-wage labor costs in order to enhance the performance of the formal sector of the economy.

With regard to education, even though Bulgaria has a well-educated and trained workforce, the country suffers from the emigration of many of its best-educated citizens. There is a serious backlog in investment in schools arising from sharp cuts in education spending in the first half of the 1990s. Further, the shortage of people with management skills and of properly trained judicial and public administration personnel, although improving, still adversely affects the performance of the corporate sector and its competitiveness prospects.

At the meeting, some of the most important, overarching issues that framed the debate concerning a roadmap for Bulgaria's development included:

3 Strengthening the administrative capacity of the social partners with particular regard to new policy areas, including employment and social inclusion, is a medium-term policy priority of the so-called roadmap for Bulgaria laid out in the European Commission's 2002 Strategy Paper and Report (2002a).

- What should be the roadmap for Bulgaria's corporate and competition policy reforms as well as for the development of the financial sector? Under what conditions can Bulgaria promote FDI inflows? What should be the extent of privatization and market liberalization?
- What challenges does the global economic environment pose for Bulgarian monetary policy and market competitiveness?
- What further efforts are needed in the areas of democracy, public administration, and human rights, and what have been the obstacles to effective implementation of reforms?
- What broader issues does Bulgaria's integration into NATO structures raise for Euro-Atlantic security and security in and around Southeastern Europe in the twenty-first century?

FDI Prospects

Arguing that foreign direct investment is a crucial factor and catalyst for transition economies, Laza Kekic, director for Central and Eastern Europe and for the country forecasts of the Economist Intelligence Unit (EIU), assessed the prospects of FDI in Bulgaria. According to the framework of the East European Investment Prospects (business environment rankings applied to the twenty-seven countries in the region) and the model of forecasting FDI, Bulgaria's end-2001 FDI stock per head of some $500 was well behind the leading FDI recipients in East Central Europe and the Baltics. However, measured as a percentage of GDP (the penetration rate of FDI), Bulgaria's 30 percent figure was similar to Central European and Baltic averages (and higher than Poland's, Slovakia's, and Slovenia's). In 2002 FDI trends in Bulgaria were not encouraging and were very worrying for the locals. FDI inflows fell sharply in the first quarter of 2002, to only $47 million from $280 million a year earlier. The main cause of lower FDI inflows was the slow progress of privatization. A further blow to hopes of attracting increased FDI was delivered when British American Tobacco announced that it would close its Bulgarian subsidiary, having decided not to take part in the sale of the state monopoly Bulgartabak. However FDI inflows were robust in 2003 and during the first three quarters of 2004.

Cautious about the positive effects of "euroization" (the adoption of the euro as the national currency) on trade, as suggested at the conference by Harvard's Alfred Schipke and Ilian Mihov of INSEAD, Kekic outlined the conditions necessary for a substantial pickup in investor interest in Bulgaria. Using a model that links FDI to measurements of the quality of a country's business environment, he stated that expected improvements in the business environment underpinned the expectation of relatively buoyant FDI in Bulgaria over the medium term – some $900 million per year. The assumptions on which these projections were based were that real GDP would grow by about 4 percent to 4.5 percent per year, which combined with appreciation against the U.S. dollar would boost dollar GDP at a rate of about 10 percent per year; that average dollar wages would also grow by 10 percent per year; that privatization policy would focus on strategic sales; and, above all, that the overall business environment would improve considerably. This was reflected in a jump of seven places in the EIU's business environment ranking (BER) between the historic and forecast periods, with Bulgaria now ranking tenth among twenty-seven countries in terms of business climate for the period 2001-05. Contrary to conventional wisdom, Kekic held that any delays in EU accession would not have a negative effect on FDI, especially if investors were confident that membership would happen at some point. In any case, one of the main attractions for investors was market access to the EU, which Bulgaria had already largely achieved prior to membership. According to the EIU's director for Eastern Europe, the arguments that EU membership is a key factor in attracting FDI are largely unsubstantiated. Many of the individual institutional reforms required for EU accession have positively influenced the business environment and thus FDI, but other factors associated with membership could actually serve to reduce FDI inflows. Kekic concluded on an optimistic note that expected improvements in the business environment would help spur substantial growth in FDI in the near future.

According to Elisabetta Falcetti, an economist with the European Bank for Reconstruction and Development (EBRD), over the past few years Bulgaria had achieved solid economic growth and made substantial progress in the area of economic reform. In her interpretation of lower net FDI inflows, which in the two years preceding the conference had fallen short of the Bulgarian current account deficit, Falcetti pointed out that access to financing was still perceived as a major obstacle to doing business in Bulgaria. Calling for renewed vigilance, she emphasized the need to improve access to financing by increasing intermediation through banks and by promoting the development of the non-banking financial sector, along with the domestic capital market in Bulgaria. The country was still lagging behind the first wave of EU accession countries in areas like corporate governance, enterprise restructuring, competition policy, and financial sector development. However, for Falcetti the full-fledged success of Bulgarian economic recovery hinged on institutional reform, as well as on important social policy reforms and combating corruption.

Global Economic Challenges

Participants at the meeting identified the Maastricht criteria for adoption of the euro and the privatization schedule as the main challenges posed by the global economic environment.

"Euroization" and Maastricht

Several speakers argued that the EU needs to reevaluate the Maastricht[4] criteria – in particular the inflation criterion – in the case of the East European applicant countries. The applicant countries tend to have higher inflation for structural reasons that have nothing to do with monetary/fiscal policy. Namely, strong catch-up productivity growth in the tradeables sector pushes up wages in both the tradeables and, through domestic competition in the labor market, in the non-tradeables sectors. This in turn pushes up non-tradeables prices (tradeables prices are governed by international competition) and thus the general price level – the so-called Balassa-Samuelson effect.

Empirical evidence on the size of the effect varies, but it seems to account for at least 1 percent to 2 percent inflation per year, and possibly more. Strict adherence to the unadjusted Maastricht criteria would have the undesirable effect of encouraging countries to suppress prices by using non-market instruments. Alternatively, it could lead to overly tight policies, which would inhibit growth.

The EU is very averse to altering the existing criteria. Its response so far has been to occasionally (but not consistently) urge the applicants to concentrate on growth and ease up if necessary on tight macroeconomic policies, even if this means some delay in satisfying the Maastricht criteria and entry into economic and monetary union (EMU). As it happens, in its July 2002 Monthly Bulletin the European Central Bank (ECB) urges the East European applicants to squeeze inflation further toward euro-zone levels. And, by way of a contradiction, it also reemphasizes that real economic convergence is now the focus of ECB's contacts with the applicants.

Appeal was also made at the conference to the controversial empirical findings of Frankel and Rose (2000) that being a member of a currency union has such a strong bearing on transaction and other costs that it triples trade with other members of the union, compared with what it would be if the trade partners had separate currencies. Subsequent research has shown the size of the impact to be considerably smaller, and it has also questioned whether there is in fact any impact at all, contending that currency unions may capture or serve as proxies for other trade-enhancing factors (such as a high degree of harmonization in legal, trade, and other practices not sufficiently accounted for in the estimates).

---

4 The Treaty on European Union, signed at Maastricht, the Netherlands, on 7 February 1992.

The themes of euroization and the relationship between exchange rate regimes and the Maastricht criteria were much discussed at the conference. These issues have been receiving a lot of attention in recent years, especially among academics (the July 2002 issue of the Economics of Transition journal carries several articles devoted to the euroization controversy, exchange rate regimes, and the implications of the Balassa-Samuelson effect). The advantages of euroization seem to loom much larger for a move from a currency board regime (the next level down in terms of the "hardness" of a peg), than from a floating regime, which is probably more difficult to leave and which also holds certain advantages for countries over a hard-peg regime (whether that regime is the currency board or adoption of another currency), such as flexibility in adjusting to external shocks.

Extraordinary as it may seem, much of the EU's opposition to euroization may boil down to confusion between euroization and joining EMU. Unilateral euroization clearly entails no decision-making rights on the euro or participation in EMU and the ECB. The ECB has no obligation to act as a lender of last resort to a country that is not a member of EMU but uses the euro (although not altogether implausibly the ECB says that it would come under strong informal and political pressure to bail out an applicant country that got into trouble). Any concern that euroization by the applicants could upset the currency markets does not seem to hold water, given the comparatively very small size of these economies. It does not make sense for an applicant country with a currency board to have to participate in the Exchange Rate Mechanism 2 (ERM2, designed for those countries with a flexible exchange rate system) before it entered EMU. It was noted that if the UK decided to join EMU it would probably not be required first to spend two years in ERM2. This could then be a precedent for applicants with a currency board. The ECB has, however, already apparently discussed the possibility of dispensing with ERM2 for those applicants that have a currency board.

Alfred Schipke, a public policy expert and former International Monetary Fund (IMF) affiliate now at Harvard University, examined the Bulgarian economy's trajectory from stabilization to growth, demonstrating that Bulgaria has made substantial strides in terms of its macroeconomic management and setting the foundation for sustainable growth and improving the standard of living. However, developments both in Brazil and in Turkey raised some concerns about the sustainability of Bulgaria's good macroeconomic performance leading up to 2002. Bulgaria, like any emerging market that has a relatively high stock of external debt, a large current account deficit, and a fixed exchange rate system, may suffer from inherent vulnerabilities and is exposed to emerging-market contagion. Given the continued uncertainties that exist in international markets, including the U.S. economy, Schipke made the controversial suggestion that currency euroization may be a viable way to do away with the current currency board system and called for a revision of Maastricht's inflation criteria. Bulgaria should consider adopting the euro unilaterally, before EU membership and certainly before it eventually joins EMU, because doing so would be an effective way of speeding up economic reforms.

Alluding to Bulgarian economic reform prospects, Schipke struck a rather more cautious note than Laza Kekic did in his assessment of Bulgaria's FDI prospects. Schipke warned of the effects of the deterioration of the external environment and lower foreign investment for fiscal management and for the control of Bulgaria's current deficit.

Martin Hallet, the European Commission's representative from the Directorate-General of Economic and Financial Affairs, outlined the achievements made possible by Bulgaria's approach to economic reform and reiterated the EU's official view that unilateral euroization would not be in compliance with the Maastricht treaty. In his response to Alfred Schipke's defense of euroization of the Bulgarian currency, Hallet stressed that "Bulgaria is not ready for such a change" and that unilateral euroization could trigger a serious economic crisis. Instead, Hallet argued, "Bulgaria should accelerate judicial and public administration reform as well as make labor market flexibility a policy priority to handle the excessively high unemployment rate." The Bulgarian program of economic reforms has aimed at macroeconomic stability and at flexible product, capital, and labor markets. As a result of the currency board arrangement, fiscal policy has been the main instrument of macroeconomic stabilization in Bulgaria. According to Hallet, other notable achievements included the reduced size of the government sector, real estate restitution, privatization, substantial domestic and foreign investment, financial sector restructuring, and a high degree of external liberalization. Yet, Hallet argued that these successes should not eclipse the need for further reforms, particularly those related to the enforceability of property rights, market regulation, the flexibility of the labor market, the deepening of capital markets, and the quality of infrastructure and human capital.

Harvard University's Jeffrey Sachs, once an advisor to former Bulgarian president Stoyanov and now a professor at Columbia University and advisor to UN Secretary General Kofi Annan on world poverty issues, engaged the audience in a lively debate over Bulgaria's development challenges. Sachs addressed three different issues: the global economic environment; lessons of Argentina for Bulgaria; and reform issues in transition economies. On Bulgaria's currency board, Sachs noted wryly that at the time that it was adopted, one of the IMF's main arguments in its favor was the "Argentine success." Much to the relief of the audience, Sachs cautioned against drawing too many direct parallels between Argentina and Bulgaria, but stated that the Argentine crisis did hold some useful lessons. Bulgaria, Sachs stressed, should not repeat Argentina's mistake, which was not moving to "dollarization" once the crisis had started. Dollarization would not have solved the serious problem of the lack of competitiveness of the economy (dollarization would have locked in the loss of competitiveness of preceding years), but it would have averted the complete collapse in the financial system and the loss of confidence that followed devaluation, confidence that will take a very long time to rebuild. Unlike Argentina, Bulgaria has a small and open economy; conducts a high share of trade with the euro area; has a plan for phasing out the currency board; has good debt management; and has prudent fiscal policy. Furthermore, dollar-euro fluctuations are overall neutral. On this last point Sachs triggered some disagreement, as the appreciation of the euro hurts Bulgaria's trade, which is still conducted in dollars. Sachs opposed unilateral euroization, stating that it would involve the extremely expensive process of printing bank notes, but he defended a quick shift to the euro in case of crisis.

According to Sachs, two main factors determined differential performance in the transition region: geography and the progress of reform. Compared to that of some of its neighbors, Bulgaria's competitiveness was still lagging, as shown in World Economic Forum competitiveness ratings, where Bulgaria ranked only fifty-ninth out of seventy-five, unlike the EIU's BER described by Laza Kekic. The BER are based on an attempt to make a forward-looking assessment of the business environment over the next five years. On this measure, Bulgaria's global rank is considerably higher than the World Economic Forum ratings (which are based on present conditions), reflecting expected improvements in Bulgaria's investment climate and the overall performance of the economy.

Berating the EU for dragging its feet on enlargement, Sachs stated that the future of the Bulgarian efforts hinged on the acceleration of the process of accession to the EU while simultaneously pushing forward further institutional reforms.

Reforms and the Privatization Schedule

Bulgaria's deputy economy minister, Sofia Kassidova, made a cogent case for Bulgaria's ability to avoid a currency board crisis. In an impressive presentation, Kassidova proposed a package of policy prescriptions that closely followed the standard World Bank/IMF package for emerging markets, with little attention to local variation or detailed consideration of the Bulgarian context. Among the measures and tasks cited, the deputy economy minister stated that Bulgaria was now working on permissible state aids policy, which do not feature special FDI incentives; energy sector reform; strengthening governance and market institutions; deepening financial institutions; the finalization of the privatization program; improved delivery of public services; the development of human capital; and judicial and administrative reform.

Krassen Stanchev, executive director of the Bulgarian Institute for Market Economy, argued, on the whole plausibly, that Bulgaria was now reasonably resilient in the face of external shocks. In a position close to that of Jeffrey Sachs, this leading local analyst argued that the country was well positioned to withstand dollar-euro fluctuations and dismissed the impact on Bulgaria of developments in other emerging markets, as suggested by Alfred Schipke. Stanchev went further to dismiss any significant impact on Bulgaria of the new post-9/11 security environment, stating that Bulgaria's reform priorities lay in the realm of domestic politics.

Stanchev suggested that, although the most strenuous period of adjustment and reorientation was over, Bulgaria still faced a number of persistent problems, one of which was the deficiency of the existing pension system. According to Stanchev, the present model of social security contributions was generating an ever-increasing gap between revenues and expenditures that the government would eventually not be able to bridge. Moreover, the pensions problem is especially thorny because, in Stanchev's opinion, any reasonable approach for dealing with the accumulation of domestic debt could damage the government's public image and result in loss of confidence.

Democracy, Public Administration, and Human Rights

The head of the European Commission delegation in Bulgaria, Dimitris Kourkoulas, noted that EU membership for Bulgaria was no longer a question of "if," but rather of "when." While Kourkoulas did not elaborate on the "when" question or what kind of roadmap the EU would provide Bulgaria after the first round of "big bang" enlargement in which Bulgaria would not be admitted, he described Bulgaria's recent progress as spectacular. He noted that Bulgaria had made rapid progress in EU accession negotiations, that it had by then provisionally closed twenty-three chapters of the acquis communautaire, and that negotiations on all remaining chapters had been opened.[5] (In fact, Bulgaria closed the last chapters and completed negotiations in April 2004.) Korkoulas stressed that Bulgaria should now focus on further reforms of public administration and human rights legislation.

Kristian Vigenin of the Bulgarian Socialist Party (BSP) explored a series of alternative scenarios regarding Bulgaria's accession to the EU and, citing a recent quip by the Bulgarian foreign minister, Solomon Passy, repeated that the expected decision on big-bang enlargement at the Copenhagen summit, leaving out only Bulgaria and Romania, would be like "ten weddings and two funerals."

The controversial issue of the Kozlodui nuclear complex (the EU wanted four out of six reactors shut down on environmental and safety grounds) did not receive much attention at the conference, even though the very next day this became a major news

---

5   The *acquis communautaire* (or community acquis) is the body of common rights and obligations that bind all member states together within the EU. Applicant countries must accept the *acquis* before joining the EU, transpose it into their national legislation, and implement it from the moment of their accession to the EU.

item, including in the international press, as, following a new IAEA report, Bulgaria said that it would refuse or challenge the EU's demands (accession requirements) on two of the reactors. Although the complex is based on Russian technology, Bulgaria refutes all comparisons with Chernobyl and claims that safety improvements in recent years mean that the complex now actually exceeds average world safety standards. Kozlodui supplies 50 percent of Bulgaria's power, electricity sales are a major export item, and there is much resentment in Bulgaria – and a profusion of conspiracy theories – concerning EU pressure. The issue promised to be key in the negotiations process.

Security Issues

Conference participants addressed the broader issues that Bulgaria's integration into NATO structures raised for Euro-Atlantic security and security in and around Southeastern Europe in the twenty-first century. These issues included Bulgaria's transition to democracy and related institutional reforms, the importance of similar transition processes in other countries in the region, and efforts to promote regional security cooperation initiatives to secure long-lasting stability.

By its history, culture, architecture, and political orientation, as well as its geography, Bulgaria is a part of Europe. Equally important, Bulgaria seeks to be integrated as fully as possible into the broader Euro-Atlantic setting. This includes both EU and NATO membership. Clearly, Bulgaria strives to become a full member of a Europe that is free, unified, and based on the institutions of democracy – a Europe that in this sense would be without precedent. According to the local perception, Bulgaria has for a decade been a regional producer rather than consumer of security, and it has provided significant assistance to NATO, especially during the Kosovo crisis. The feeling at the meeting, especially among the audience, was that it was time for Western institutions in general and the EU in particular to compensate Bulgaria through extensive financial assistance in its transition to democratic rule and the road toward accession.

Robert Pfaltzgraff, president of the Institute of Foreign Policy Analysis, and Lybomir Ivanov, Bulgaria's deputy foreign minister, commented on Bulgarian foreign and defense policies. Robert Pfaltzgraff praised Bulgaria's security policy reforms and its progress toward meeting NATO standards, stating that Bulgaria belonged in NATO. According to this security expert, the most important challenge for new NATO members will be to adapt to an Alliance that is undergoing vast and rapid change itself, especially in response to the events of September 11, 2001, and the conflict in Iraq. Although NATO has been reinventing itself throughout its more than fifty-year history, the war against terrorism has dramatically transformed NATO priorities and shaped discussions within the Alliance. The Alliance that the new members will be joining will be in the midst of its own rapid change, as the November 2002 Prague Summit and subsequent events related to the crisis over Iraq have revealed.

How the transatlantic relationship will evolve will depend on the extent to which the United States and Europe view each other as partners or rivals. For the United States the good news is that the eagerness of would-be NATO members to join the Alliance is related to the importance that they attach to a transatlantic link with the United States. For NATO's newer members, however, it will be essential also to strengthen their relationships within Europe. It is to be hoped that a more unified Europe will not pose a threat to the transatlantic relationship. Unfortunately, there is no single, clear-cut solution that will ensure that Europe becomes a partner rather than a rival to the United States.

Bulgaria and its neighbors need to contend with the challenge of reconciling their interests within Europe and in the transatlantic relationship. How those interests are formulated and harmonized will have important implications for twenty-first-century institutions and relationships within and outside Europe. What should be obvious on both sides of the Atlantic is the extent to which the Euro-Atlantic area constitutes a region of stability in a world of crisis and turmoil. That the United States' and Europe's ability to combat threats emanating from other regions will be strengthened by partnership and threatened by rivalry should be self-evident.

For Dr. Pfaltzgraff, the idea that "Old Europe" and "New Europe" could be brought into transatlantic harmony with the United States was doubtful, especially if the goal of "Old Europe," led by France, was to diminish the position of the United States. Such a tactic appeared both shortsighted and counterproductive, and its immediate effect was to divide Europe. Its longer-term consequence could be to weaken necessary collective efforts to wage war against terrorism in a setting in which Europe, no less than the United States, was likely to be a terrorist target.

Deputy Minister Ivanov had to face some difficult questions. Bulgaria's defense budget, at 3.1 percent of GDP in 2002, was just about the highest in Europe in proportional terms, and the 2003 budget preserved this share. In addressing the issue the minister said that this was indeed a burden, but that Bulgaria had international obligations to meet, which would affect minimum nominal expenditures (low GDP meant that defense expenditures represented a relatively high share of GDP). Although the minister tried to put the best spin possible on the issue he admitted that Bulgaria faced great problems because of lags in the development of trade infrastructure and also because of its relative isolation. The twenty-year plans to build a second bridge connecting Bulgaria with Romania had not been really finalized. A planned highway to the southern Serbian city of Nis was also in trouble and not a priority for the Yugoslav government, which was emphasizing north-south links. Further, Corridor 8 links with Macedonia had been running into trouble, and the minister also referred to efforts to alleviate bottlenecks on the border with Greece and the government's plans to open three new border crossings.

In closing, the conference highlighted the overall success of Bulgaria's efforts, success that continues into 2005. Taken together the policy reforms attest to the strong commitment of the Bulgarian leadership to the modernization of the country. The sustained period of economic and political stability is unprecedented for a country in economic transition, and this stability does not appear threatened in the near future. Macroeconomic stability has allowed Bulgaria to address substantial remaining needs in restructuring and institutional development, and it is reasonable to expect improvements in output and living standards and continued reform of the financial markets. Further, substantial foreign direct investment, continued rapid privatization, and the fostering of a vibrant SME sector can help to accelerate restructuring and alleviate the implied temporary social costs.

The success of Bulgaria's economic policy should allow the government to meet the enormous challenges that remain: the need for further efforts in human rights; full implementation of the rule of law; administrative and judicial reform; and investments in education and the development of human capital.

Special thanks for their fundamental assistance in securing the participation of Bulgarian senior officials go to Maxim Behar and Maria Zhekova, of M3 Communications, Bulgaria.

References

Economics of Transition 10, no. 2 (July 2002): 235-523.

EIU. 2005. *Country report Bulgaria*. January.

European Central Bank. 2002. *Monthly Bulletin*. July.

European Commission. 2002b. *Towards the enlarged union: Strategy paper and report of the European Commission on the progress towards accession by each of the candidate countries.* [SEC (2002) 1400 1412], Brussels (October). http://europa.eu.int/comm/enlargement/report2002/strategy_en.pdf.

———. 2002a. 2002 *Regular report on Bulgaria's progress towards accession* {COM(2002) 700 final}, Brussels (October).

———. 2003. 2003 *Regular report on Bulgaria's progress towards accession*. http://europa.eu.int/comm/enlargement/report_2003/pdf/rr_bg_final.pdf.

———. 2004. *2004 Regular Report on Bulgaria's progress Towards Accession*. http://europa.eu.int/comm/enlargement/report_2004/pdf/rr_bg_2004_en.pdf.

Frankel, Jeffrey A., and Andrew K. Rose. 2000. Estimating the effects of currency unions on trade and output. Working Paper 7857, National Bureau of Economic Research (August).

2 Welcoming Address

Meglena Kuneva, Minister of European Affairs, Republic of Bulgaria

Edited transcript of Minister Kuneva's address to the conference

Ladies and Gentlemen,
Your Excellencies,

Allow me to greet you wholeheartedly on the occasion of the opening of the international conference, Bulgaria in Europe, as well as to thank the organizers for their wonderful idea and its implementation.

Your efforts to involve Bulgarian society in this long-term reform project called the European Union do deserve high appreciation and gratitude. Especially now that Bulgaria is at a turning point in its EU accession negotiations, since at the moment we are negotiating the enforcement of EU single market rules in Bulgaria and are laying the foundation for the economic accession of our country into the European Union.

I am glad to report to you that Bulgaria has opened all the thirty negotiation chapters of the *acquis communautaire* and closed twenty of them, which is two-thirds of the total. Our goal is to end negotiations by the end of 2003.[1] This date, set in the government strategy for acceleration of EU negotiations, stems from an in-depth analysis of the actual capacity of our country.

The success of the country is a result of our efforts to fulfill the conditions and prepare Bulgaria for its future membership in the EU, as we believe that our country will very soon take its indisputable place among the united family of European nations.

Our country is an inseparable part of the united Europe concept because the idea for a large-scale EU expansion means, for all practical purposes, permanent peace on the continent, democracy, rule of law, free market economy, and a worthy life for each citizen. These values are shared by modern democratic Bulgaria.

---

1   In June 2004 Bulgaria and the EU concluded the country's accession negotiations with the closing of the final two chapters of the *acquis communautaire*.

In this respect I take the motto and title of your conference, "Bulgaria in Europe," not as an appeal but as a confirmation.

I do hope that we will work together in the future and I wish useful work to the conference.

3 The Bulgarian Developmental Challenge: Policy Priorities and the Reform Effort

By Nikolay Vassilev, Deputy Prime Minister and Minister of the Economy, Republic of Bulgaria

Edited and updated paper based on the conference

The Bulgarian economy has undergone substantial changes since the end of the Second World War. Under the postwar regime of central planning, Bulgaria transformed its mostly agrarian economy into an industrial one, becoming an economic leader among the socialist countries of Central and Eastern Europe. The inefficient use and mismanagement of resources during this era led to the eventual collapse of central planning across these countries and created the conditions for another transition in Bulgaria, this time to a free market economy. The collapse of the communist regimes in the former Soviet Union and in some of the Central and East European nations in the late 1980s and early 1990s set the stage for the emergence of the grassroots of capitalist society in the newly democratic Bulgaria.

The Bulgarian economy went through several turbulent years in the first half of the 1990s, when the most basic structures of capitalism were being established. Following a period of hyperinflation, collapsing currency, and rising unemployment, however, the free market reforms in Bulgaria started in earnest in the late 1990s. Having achieved solid economic growth, low inflation, a stable currency, and falling unemployment since the late 1990s, Bulgaria has earned international respect. Bulgaria is an active member of the United Nations Security Council, a new member of NATO, a candidate for EU membership, and a country with a functioning market economy recognized by both the European Commission and the United States. Bulgaria's role in the international community is becoming more active, especially after its full support of the United States during the disarmament of Iraq. Together with its numerous friends in the global democratic community, Bulgaria hopes to play a key role in the reconstruction and rebuilding of a democratic Iraq. Bulgaria has friendly relations with all of its neighbors and it is an active member of the World Trade Organization (WTO) and the Central European Free Trade Association (CEFTA).

The performance of the Bulgarian economy over the past several years has been nothing short of miraculous. The economy grew by 4.9 percent in 2002 after a gross domestic product growth of 4.1 percent and 5.4 percent respectively in the preceding two years. In 2003 and 2004, real GDP grew by 4.5 percent and 5.6 percent, respectively. Inflation in 2004 increased to 6.1 percent from 2.3 percent in 2003, although inflation is expected to decline to 4.5 percent for 2005. Industrial production and sales grew by 9.7 percent year-on-year in July 2005, while exports grew by 12 percent year-on-year in the second quarter of 2005. The vigorous growth of the economy has resulted in a substantial drop in unemployment, with the jobless rate in the second quarter of 2005 at 10 percent, down from 14.1 percent in the first quarter of 2004. Rises in employment and economic activity have been achieved despite anemic growth in Europe. Bulgaria's current and trade account deficits widened between the first and second quarters of 2005, although its foreign exchange reserves increased slightly during the same period. Following a strong 2004, the country's tourism revenue for the first seven months of 2005 rose by 10.2 percent. While Bulgaria has achieved solid economic growth since 1998, the country aims to continue to have one of the highest gross domestic product growth rates in Europe and to become an economic tiger in the Balkans.

The economic progress enjoyed by Bulgaria over the past several years has received wide recognition with most of the international credit rating agencies. Moody's, Standard and Poor's, Fitch IBCA, and the Japan Credit Rating Agency have all raised Bulgaria's credit rating on several occasions since 2001. The business and free-market-oriented efforts of the Bulgarian government have led to a rapid reduction of state participation in the national economy. The private sector accounted for 75 percent of GDP in 2004, with the largest share of output attributable to service sector activity. Bulgaria's financial sector has become very dynamic and well developed, with all of the state banks either privatized or close to being so. It is Bulgaria's aim to have better developed, highly capitalized markets, with a higher degree of liquidity. Although still in its infancy, Bulgaria's equity index, the Sofix, rose by over 630 percent in the period between the start of April 2002 and the end of September 2005.

The present government of Bulgaria, which stepped into office in June 2001, has embarked on an ambitious and sweeping economic reform program. One of its key priorities is to continue working closely with multinational organizations such as the International Monetary Fund (IMF), the World Bank, and the European Bank of Reconstruction and Development (EBRD), whose support has proven invaluable to the nation over the past several years. In February 2002, the IMF approved a two-year standby facility for Bulgaria worth SDR 250 million[1], while the World Bank has adopted a supporting strategy worth $750 million over the 2002-05 period The EBRD has separately launched a $500 million private sector financing program.

---

1   The SDR, or special drawing right, is an international reserve asset created by the IMF.

A key priority of the Bulgarian government is to maintain the currency board arrangement by keeping the peg between the Bulgarian lev and the euro until entry into the European Union, which is scheduled for 2007. The currency board, adopted in 1997, has had a pronounced stabilizing effect on the Bulgarian economy, reducing inflation – recently into the low single digits – while not acting as a brake to credit expansion. Interest rates have fallen sharply and the premium over European borrowing costs has narrowed significantly, exemplifying the growing degree of investor confidence in the macroeconomic stability enjoyed by Bulgaria.

Among the key pending reform initiatives of the Bulgarian government is the completion of the privatization of large state-owned enterprises, which it hopes to accomplish in full by the end of its mandate. The government has already privatized most of the banking sector and has also sold off 67-percent stakes in Bulgaria's seven regional power distribution companies. In 2005 Bulgaria may also succeed in privatizing Bulgartabac, the state tobacco company, as well as Bulgargaz, the gas company.

Eradicating corruption and reducing bureaucracy to a minimum also remain among the key challenges faced by the Bulgarian government. According to Transparency International, between 1998 and 2001 Bulgaria moved from sixty-sixth to forty-seventh place on the global corruption index, illustrating a decisive reduction in corruption, a trend that the current government is determined to maintain and accelerate up until the mid-2005 elections. In terms of the Bulgarian strategy for the reduction of bureaucracy, the government has identified 194 licensing and permit regimes for either complete eradication or substantial simplification. One hundred seven regimes are already being reformed and the others will either be amended or removed altogether.

Increasing investment activity in the Bulgarian economy remains a priority, with the attraction of foreign direct investment (FDI) standing as one of the nation's main ambitions. The flow of foreign capital into Bulgaria will not only serve to improve productivity, increase living standards, and lower unemployment; it will also help substantially with Bulgaria's efforts to modernize the economy, introduce twenty-first-century business practices, and incorporate cutting-edge technology into production processes. The average annual inflow of foreign direct investment between 1997 and 2004 was over $1.1 billion, a figure that was partly helped by privatization receipts. The deterioration of the global investment climate over 2001 led to some decline in the inflows of FDI, yet the government's economic team launched efforts to reverse these signs of moderation in investment. In addition to Bulgaria's advantage of having some of the lowest costs associated with doing business in Europe, the nation's liberalized access to markets with over 560 million consumers, its recent NATO membership and forthcoming EU membership, its robust legal framework focused on attracting and protecting foreign investment, its rapidly improving business climate, and its superb academic and vocational training all make the country a highly attractive destination for foreign investment projects.

Beyond attracting high-quality FDI, the Bulgarian government aims to accelerate the organic growth of the economy by promoting the development of the large, medium, and small-sized enterprise sectors. A number of initiatives have been taken to stimulate small business in Bulgaria. The country has secured approval for the establishment of a microcredit guarantee fund and has approved the concept of and a strategy for a one-stop-shop administrative management of small and medium-sized enterprise (SME) issues. The latest initiative in the SME sector is the establishment of a private equity fund with state participation providing up to LV100 million (approximately €50 million) of government money. The fund will be co-financed by the private sector and will be managed on a purely commercial basis by a reputable international private equity specialist, targeting an investment portfolio focused on the small and medium-sized enterprise sector.

Bulgaria's economic development program has also emphasized the creation of industrial regions, featuring preferential treatment for investment projects that create new employment and new business opportunities. Bulgaria's focus remains on cultivating an entrepreneurial culture and on promoting a business-friendly tax environment. Bulgaria has introduced a new fiscal structure featuring some of the lowest business and personal taxes in Europe. Bulgarian businesses enjoy a corporate tax rate as low as 23.5 percent, with zero taxation in areas with high unemployment. The nation's focus on stimulating the high technology sector of the economy has prompted Bulgaria to reduce its depreciation rates further, to two years for computer equipment and to just over three years for investment equipment. The total tax burden in the economy fell from 34.2 percent of GDP in 2000 to 31.6 percent of GDP in 2002, and in 2005 the tax on corporate profits will be cut from 19.5 percent to 15 percent. This has been achieved without compromising Bulgaria's strategy for fiscal austerity and prudence. The national budget deficit remains one of the lowest in Europe. Capital gains and interest income taxes have been abolished and personal taxation has been lowered substantially. Individuals whose income was previously in the 22 percent, 26, percent, or 29 percent tax brackets will see their tax rates in 2005 fall to 20 percent, 22 percent, and 24 percent, respectively. The government's focus on promoting the business sector has found many expressions, including planned changes to the legislature that will accelerate bankruptcy procedures from four years to just three months, making them among the fastest in the world. In order to facilitate the development of asset markets and business planning, the government's economic team established a real-estate market index in 2002, which showed a rise in property values of nearly 4.5 percent between August 2002 and March 2003. For the first six months of 2005, this index grew by 14 percent.

The government realizes that the economic success of Bulgaria depends as much on creating the right structures for free economic activity as it does on developing the country's biggest asset – its people. Various programs have been enacted for job creation and for the enhancement of labor productivity. The government is an ardent supporter of business education and has a particularly strong focus on developing the young generation of Bulgarians. Bulgaria has created an executive MBA program at the American University of Bulgaria, organized chartered financial analyst (CFA) courses, and established the structures necessary for facilitating internships for bright, young Bulgarians in some of the largest and best-run business organizations in the world. In a program that has achieved significant progress, the government has focused on bringing young, Western-educated Bulgarians working abroad back to Bulgaria. A large portion of the government's economic team consists of individuals with significant investment banking experience in the City of London and on Wall Street. In short, the key priorities of the government's economic team are to steer the economy toward transparency, to achieve vigorous business development, to ensure minimal government intervention in the economic life of the country, to secure high tax compliance, to create high rates of foreign and domestic investment, and to fully eradicate economic crime.

4 The Bulgarian Currency Board and Monetary Policy Reform: Lessons from the Case of Argentina

By Jeffrey Sachs, Galen L. Stone Professor of International Trade, Harvard University, and Director of the Center for International Development, Harvard University

Edited transcript of Professor Sachs's presentation at the conference

The United States is going through the same kind of bubble economy that afflicted so many other economies during the 1990s. Just as we had the boom and bust in East Asia, just as we had the boom and bust in some other economies in Central Europe and in Latin America, the United States is going through a cycle in which there is a huge flow of funds into investments in the United States, particularly in the information technology sector. Of course there was a bubble in the stock market, which led to valuations of shares that were perhaps five times more than justified, if not beyond that, and what we are experiencing now is the end of that bubble.

It is an interesting question how in the world's most sophisticated financial market, the most egregious kind of mistakes were made again. We know that capitalism is unstable, and John Maynard Keynes told us seventy-five years ago how financial markets tend to exaggerate developments significantly. Consistent with this lesson, the boom-and-bust cycle that occurred in supposedly emerging markets and less sophisticated economies hit the United States. The United States has now experienced, after the increase of wealth in the U.S. stock market, which was about $10 trillion, a loss of perhaps $3 trillion or $4 trillion in the last year as a result of the collapse of the bubble, and we are likely to experience more. What has obviously happened as well is that the huge flow of investments into the United States is partly reversing itself, seen in the fact that the dollar, which like the stock market got hugely overvalued relative to the euro – probably 30 percent overvalued at $0.82 per euro – has now started to depreciate and the euro and the dollar are approximately at parity.[1]

The big question for the United States and for Europe is the extent to which the bursting of the bubble could lead to a financial calamity and even a deepening

---

1   As of October 24, 2005, the exchange rate was nearly $1.20 per euro.

recession, and there is one basic point to understand here. When a stock market bubble collapses, as is happening in the United States, there are two kinds of risks. The first risk is that there is a loss of confidence among consumers and investors, which leads to a decline of consumption and investment spending. And that is not just a matter of loss of confidence but of the loss of wealth that has come with the decline of the stock market. The second risk is that the financial system goes into crisis as a result of the declining stock market prices. This can happen if the companies that are failing owe a lot of money to the banks and then the banks start to have a major balance-sheet crisis. These are the two kinds of risks that we need to analyze in the U.S. context. The U.S. banking system is probably strong enough that it will not fall into crisis as a result of this bursting of the bubble. While nobody can be sure of that, if the U.S. banking sector remains adequately strong, then the decline of the stock market will lead to a slowdown of U.S. growth but probably not to an open recession and certainly not a depression. So some people say that the United States is now going to experience what Japan experienced in the 1990s or even, one could say, what Bulgaria experienced in the mid-1990s, which was a bubble that collapsed and was followed by a prolonged crisis. From this vantage point, however, that scenario seems unlikely, because the real economy, especially the financial system and the banking system, is probably strong enough to weather this shock, unlike in Japan, where the end of the Japanese bubble at the end of the 1980s actually led to a banking sector crisis, or in Bulgaria where the crisis in the mid-1990s led to a collapse of the banking sector. It is also important to understand, since some people mention it, that in the Great Depression the stock market crash of 1929 was not the main cause of the depression itself; rather, the cause of the Great Depression was the banking crisis that followed the stock market crash. So, if the United States can avoid a banking crisis as a result of this boom and bust on the stock market, it will probably avoid calamity. That is good news for the whole world, because if the United States experienced a banking sector crisis, this would be a major threat for the world economy. Many people have lost a lot of money, which they gained very, very quickly on paper and which now has disappeared. Still, it does not appear that this will lead to a catastrophe in the U.S. economy itself. What the United States is experiencing is the end of euphoria. Much criminal behavior is being uncovered that took place during the boom and bust episode. This was true in Bulgaria, in Japan, and in East Asia. A speculative bubble that attracts huge amounts of money irrationally into the markets is an invitation for legal abuse and criminality. This was the case in the United States just as it was in other countries.

As for Argentina, that country is experiencing a real crisis. It is much deeper than the U.S. crisis. This is interesting because in the mid-1990s, when Bulgaria joined the currency board system, the IMF encouraged the government to join because of the success of the Argentine currency board, and memos were written saying that the reason the IMF was insisting on this in Bulgaria was the Argentine success story. And so probably there are some questions in Argentina's crisis, the very deepest in the world, about what the practical implications might be, or the practical lessons might be, for the currency board system itself. The currency board system is a fragile system, and even in the case of Bulgaria there were safer ways to proceed. In the case of Argentina it was clear that having adopted a currency board in April 1991, pegging the Argentine peso one to one with the U.S. dollar, Argentina got into a competitiveness crisis by the mid- to late 1990s. That competitiveness crisis was the combination of the currency board's rigid system together with the lack of competitiveness in the Argentine economy. It is important to understand very briefly what happened in Argentina, so that the same problems don't arise in Bulgaria. There is no reason however to believe that Bulgaria would have to experience the kind of crisis that Argentina did. There is a much simpler and safer route for Bulgaria, so Argentina's crisis should not be seen in any way as a predictor for Bulgaria, but it does have a lesson for Bulgaria.

By the late 1990s the Argentine economy was no longer competitive. The currency was too strong, and there were widespread expectations that it would have to be devalued. The Argentine government said that it had a currency board and so would never devalue the currency. However, Argentine investors did not believe the government and they began withdrawing funds from the Argentine banking system and stopped investing in Argentine government bonds. In 2000 and 2001 this withdrawal of money from the banking system led to a severe liquidity crisis, where the banks became illiquid. The central bank could not provide liquidity for the commercial banks because that would have meant a loss of dollar reserves and could have led to the collapse of the currency board itself. The more illiquid the banks became, the more it was expected that Argentina would have to devalue the currency.

Finally, in late 2001, Argentina faced a bank panic, a massive run on the commercial banks. At this point the government made a very bad decision: it froze the accounts in the banking sector and told the depositors that they could not withdraw their money. This of course led to a political crisis and the government of President de La Rua collapsed. The new government came in and it had a choice about what to do: it decided that it would devalue the currency, even though it had promised the Argentine public that it would never devalue the currency. But it did devalue the currency, which led to a crisis in which the Argentine people demanded even faster withdrawals from the banking sector, but they were not allowed to get their money out because their deposits were frozen in the banking sector. This continues to be the situation today. Deposits are frozen, spending by the public and by businesses has collapsed, people cannot get their money out, and they have stopped paying taxes. Consequently the budget is in big deficit and the currency is rapidly losing value. This may sound somewhat familiar to the Bulgarian crisis of the mid-1990s. In any event, what Argentina has now faced is the full collapse of its banking sector, the collapse of its currency board, and the collapse of confidence in the country. Since confidence in the government itself has collapsed completely, new elections will have to be held soon.

What is the lesson for Bulgaria? It certainly isn't that just because Argentina had a crisis like this, any other currency board system necessarily will have a crisis. But it is important to understand that even a currency board system can have a loss of confidence, in which people believe that the currency value will change through devaluation. What Argentina should have done, when the loss of confidence occurred, was to "dollarize" the economy. In 2001, Argentina should simply have abandoned the Argentine peso as a national currency and gone entirely to the U.S. dollar on which its currency was based. In the analogy with Bulgaria, if ever there were a crisis of confidence about the currency board, the right response would simply be to introduce the euro and finish the process, so that there would be no loss to confidence in the currency board. If Argentina had done this, it would have avoided the kind of confidence crisis that it has in fact now endured. Unfortunately both the Argentine government and the IMF were against "dollarization." At least the Argentines were and the IMF was very ambiguous and not clear about it. But in the case of Bulgaria it does seem that there is a very clear exit strategy if one is needed from the currency board and that is simply to introduce the euro and to end the crisis in that way. What the Argentine example illustrates is that moving from a currency board back to a floating currency is a very dangerous, unwise, expensive, and crisis-ridden process.

The main point is that the Argentine crisis showed the instability of this kind of currency board arrangement. It is to be hoped that the IMF is out of the business of advising on such an arrangement in the future because it is not a very wise arrangement. Finally, with regard to Bulgaria's own economic strategy, it is clear that for transition economies two factors have been most important. One is the quality of the economic reform itself and the second is the geography of the country. Countries whose territory is close to the European Union have outperformed countries that are farther away. This is because the closer countries have been able to attract foreign direct investment and have generally been able to have greater expansion of international trade than countries like Bulgaria, which are some distance away. Of course Bulgaria and other countries in the Balkans also suffered from the Yugoslav wars, which were a major barrier to foreign investment and a major barrier to trade for many, many years. Both of these factors, the quality of policy and geography, are temporary factors in the sense that all of the countries in Central and Eastern Europe ought to be able to achieve good economic progress by means of full integration into Europe.

The disappointment of the process of reform, beyond the huge disappointment of the disasters in Yugoslavia, is the fact that the integration of Central and Eastern Europe into the European Union is taking such a long time. This is making the reform process harder, not easier, in Central and Eastern Europe. We now understand that so much of the delay is really not the problem of Central and Eastern Europe, it is the problem of Western Europe. It is the problem of the very strong vested interest groups in agriculture and in other areas that have made it difficult for Western European countries to speed the membership. It all comes down to money and the money has been mainly the problem in Western Europe, of the Common Agricultural Policy and other vested interested groups in Western Europe that have made things more difficult than they need to be. The basic strategy for Central and Eastern Europe should be to accede to the European Union. Western Europe has been gambling badly by delaying this process, and speeding the process of accession of the East European countries would be beneficial for both sides. It is also true that Bulgaria, like other countries in the region, has considerable reform work still left to do. This has been studied, of course, at Harvard every year. The World Economic Forum produced the Global Competitiveness Report, and this year's report showed again that unfortunately Bulgaria still ranks only fifty-ninth out of seventy-five countries in overall competitiveness.

Competitiveness can be seen as having three dimensions, all reflecting some policy choices. The first is the quality of public institutions, the second is the macroeconomic environment, and the third is the level of technology. In each of these dimensions, Bulgaria ranks on the low side. In the quality of public institutions, it ranks fifty-first out of seventy-five countries, in the macroeconomic environment it ranks fifty-ninth, and in level of technology it ranks fiftieth. In each of these cases, however, there are positive signs. For example, Bulgaria shows up as having very good higher education, and some good prospects for high technology, but this is not being realized today. On the macroeconomic environment, the biggest problem has been the weakness of the banking system; still, on the other hand the budget has looked pretty good. The point is that Bulgaria still ranks rather low in the overall competitiveness. That combined with the geographical difficulties has certainly made it tougher for Bulgaria, than, for example, Poland, Hungary, or the Czech Republic, to be able to get fully engaged in economic growth in the last ten years. The way forward certainly is to hasten accession to the European Union and combine that with further institutional reforms within Bulgaria.

5 Prospects for Foreign Direct Investment in Bulgaria

Laza Kekic, Director for Central and Eastern Europe & for Country Forecasts, Economist Intelligence Unit

Foreign direct investment (FDI) has long been seen as a crucial factor and catalyst in the transition to market economies. FDI in transition economies grew very slowly in the early 1990s. In fact, with few exceptions, inflows were generally disappointing, falling far short of expectations. However, since the mid-1990s, FDI flows to the region increased sharply. In addition to Hungary, the Czech Republic and Poland began to attract relatively large inflows from the middle of the decade, resulting in a high concentration of FDI in these three countries. FDI inflows into the region took off in 1995, more than doubling over the previous year's total. After falling back slightly again in 1996, they increased to $29 billion in 2000 and to over $52 billion in 2004.

The acceleration of privatization and the generally improving economic and political conditions in other transition economies boosted their FDI inflows and began to result in a somewhat more even geographical distribution. FDI has also responded to the considerable improvement in the East European investment climate in recent years. The early reformers of the countries of Central Europe led the way in the early 1990s in adopting far-reaching stabilization, liberalization and privatization programs. Reform in Russia and other republics of the former Soviet Union, as well as in the Balkans, has been much more uneven and subject to periodic reversals, but even in these sub-regions significant progress is now being made.

The global financial crises of 1997-98 had only a limited impact on FDI in the transition economies. In fact, total inflows continued to rise, a reflection of both the long-term planning horizon of foreign direct investors and the more immediate opportunities presented by depressed asset prices. Foreign investors remained interested in acquiring strategic assets, especially in telecommunications companies. FDI into Russia did fall sharply in the wake of the 1998 ruble crisis, which greatly exacerbated an unfavorable investment climate. The Kosovo conflict also discouraged investment in the Balkans, at least temporarily. Despite emerging-market turbulence, FDI inflows into the transition region as a whole reached high levels in 1999-2001. So far the available evidence does not suggest that the events of September 11, 2001, have had much of an impact.

FDI Trends in Bulgaria

Bulgaria's record in attracting FDI was very disappointing in the initial period of its transition, owing to a poor business environment, macroeconomic and political

Table 1. Foreign direct investment inflows ($ million)

	1992	1993	1994	1995	1996	1997	1998	1999	2000	2001	2002	2003	2004
East Central Europe	***3,372***	***5,031***	***4,285***	***11,417***	***9,746***	***10,857***	***14,186***	***17,352***	***19,288***	***17,277***	***21,341***	***9,242***	***16,488***
Czech Republic	1,004	654	878	2,568	1,435	1,286	3,700	6,313	4,987	5,641	8,497	2,021	4,454
Hungary	1,479	2,350	1,145	4,804	3,289	4,155	3,343	3,308	2,770	3,944	3,013	2,202	4,130
Poland	678	1,715	1,875	3,659	4,498	4,908	6,365	7,270	9,343	5,714	4,131	4,123	6,288
Slovakia	100	199	270	236	351	174	562	354	2,052	1,475	4,014	559	1,100
Slovenia	111	113	117	150	173	334	216	107	136	503	1,686	337	516
Balkans	***275***	***487***	***809***	***823***	***1,232***	***3,188***	***3,936***	***3,686***	***3,613***	***4,240***	***4,305***	***8,089***	***9,593***
Albania	20	58	53	70	90	48	45	41	143	207	135	178	n.a.
Bosnia and Herzegovina	n.a.	n.a	n.a	n.a	n.a	n.a	67	177	146	118	268	382	613
Bulgaria	**34**	**102**	**211**	**163**	**256**	**636**	**620**	**819**	**1,002**	**813**	**905**	**2,097**	**2,488**
Croatia	16	120	117	114	511	533	932	1,464	1,085	1,338	1,213	2,133	1,176
Macedonia	2	17	24	12	11	16	128	32	175	442	78	95	n.a.
Romania	77	94	341	419	263	1,215	2,031	1,041	1,037	1,157	1,144	1,844	5,316
Yugoslavia	126	96	63	45	102	740	113	112	25	165	562	1,360	n.a.
Baltics	***121***	***237***	***459***	***455***	***684***	***1,142***	***1,864***	***1,140***	***1,179***	***1,120***	***1,251***	***1,398***	***2,469***
Estonia	82	162	214	202	150	266	581	305	387	542	285	919	1,049
Latvia	29	45	214	180	382	521	357	348	413	132	254	300	647
Lithuania	10	30	31	73	152	355	926	487	379	446	712	179	773

Table 1. Foreign direct investment inflows ($ million) *continued*

	1992	1993	1994	1995	1996	1997	1998	1999	2000	2001	2002	2003	2004
Former Soviet Republics	**1,779**	**1,876**	**1,771**	**4,023**	**5,321**	**9,038**	**6,781**	**6,863**	**5,428**	**7,157**	**8,899**	**15,689**	**23,628**
Russia	1,454	1,211	690	2,065	2,579	4,864	2,764	3,309	2,713	2,748	3,461	7,958	12,479
Ukraine	170	198	159	267	521	623	743	496	595	792	693	1,424	1,715
Belarus	7	18	11	15	105	352	203	444	119	96	247	172	169
Moldova	17	14	12	26	24	79	76	38	127	53	132	71	88
Armenia	2	1	8	25	18	52	221	122	104	70	111	121	219
Azerbaijan	0	60	22	330	627	1,115	1,023	510	130	227	1,392	3,285	3,556
Georgia	0	0	8	6	40	243	265	82	131	110	167	339	499
Kazakhstan	100	228	635	964	1,137	1,321	1,151	1,587	1,283	2,835	2,590	2,088	4,269
Kyrgyz Republic	0	10	38	96	47	84	109	44	-2	5	5	46	175
Tajikistan	9	9	12	20	25	30	24	21	22	20	36	32	272
Turkmenistan	11	79	103	233	108	108	62	89	131	130	n.a.	n.a.	n.a.
Uzbekistan	9	48	73	-24	90	167	140	121	75	71	65	153	187
Eastern Europe total	**5,547**	**7,631**	**7,324**	**16,718**	**16,984**	**24,225**	**26,767**	**29,041**	**29,508**	**29,794**	**35,796**	**34,418**	**52,178**

Sources: IMF; UNCTAD; EIU national statistics

instability, ineffective public administration, a harsh tax regime, and the unpredict-ability of foreign investment rules. An additional factor deterring foreign investors was the regional instability connected to conflicts in the former Yugoslavia. Initially, privatization was slow: the most attractive industrial enterprises were not offered for sale until 1997 or later, and as of 2002 the privatization of utilities and telecoms had not yet taken off. However, as of December 2004, 57 percent of state enterprise assets had been sold. This total represented 85 percent of the assets expected to undergo privatization. In the energy sector, the sale of 67-percent stakes in Bulgaria's seven regional power distribution companies was completed in 2004. Also, in June 2004 a 65-percent stake in the national telecommunications company, the Bulgarian Tele-communications Company, was transferred to Viva Ventures.

According to the InvestBulgaria Agency (formerly the Bulgarian Foreign Investment Agency, or FIA), cumulative foreign direct investment inflows in 1992-2004 were $10.1 billion, with privatization accounting for $3.2 billion, or 31 percent of the total.

At end-2004, according to the balance of payments (central bank/IMF) data, FDI per head for the Balkans was the third highest, at $863, behind that for East Central Europe ($2,430) and the Baltics ($1,908), but ahead of that for the Former Soviet Union ($354). Measured as a percentage of GDP (the penetration rate of FDI), how-ever, Bulgaria's 42.1 percent exceeded both the East Central European average and the Baltic average. Cumulative figures mask an acceleration of FDI during the 2000-04 period. According to the InvestBulgaria data, $7.3 billion of the $10.1 billion dates from the period since the start of 2000, almost half of it in the years 2002-04.

Table 2. FDI stocks, end-2004 (cumulative FDI inflows 1992-2004)

	FDI stock ($ billion)	FDI stock per head ($)	FDI stock, % of GDP		FDI stock ($ billion)	FDI stock per head ($)	FDI stock, % of GDP
East Central Europe	159.9	2,430	30.6	*Former Soviet reps.*	98.3	354	13.1
Czech Republic	43.4	4,266	40.6	Russia	48.3	338	8.3
Hungary	39.9	3,965	40.1	Ukraine	8.4	175	12.9
Poland	60.6	1,587	25.1	Belarus	2.0	199	8.6
Slovakia	11.4	2,123	27.9	Moldova	0.8	179	29.2
Slovenia	4.5	2,255	14.0	Armenia	1.1	352	30.3
Balkans	44.3	863	26.0	Azerbaijan	12.3	1,483	144.0
Albania	1.1	343	19.1	Georgia	1.9	418	37.1
Bosnia and Herzegovina	1.8	462	21.8	Kazakhstan	20.2	1,350	49.6
Bulgaria	*10.1*	*1,304*	*42.1*	Kyrgyz Rep.	0.7	129	29.8
Croatia	10.8	2,385	31.4	Tajikistan	0.5	83	25.6
Macedonia	1.0	504	22.1	Turkmenistan	1.1	223	30.6
Romania	16.0	731	21.8	Uzbekistan	1.2	45	9.8
Yugoslavia	3.5	431	17	*Eastern Europe*	315.9	786	21.2
Baltics	13.5	1,908	29.0				
Estonia	5.1	3,825	48.0				
Latvia	3.8	1,660	28.0				
Lithuania	159.9	2,430	30.6				

Sources: IMF; UNCTAD; EIU national statistics, World Development Indicators. For countries that did not have FDI data for 2004, the most recent year for which data was available was used for calculating cumulative FDI, as well as FDI stock per

In general, significant inflows of FDI have been too recent to have yet had a significant impact on areas such as Bulgaria's domestic suppliers, employment, labor skills, and technology levels. FDI inflows averaged more than 40 percent of fixed investment in 1997-2000. Although a large portion of inflows has been in the form of privatization receipts, and has thus not yet made a direct contribution to increasing the capital stock, the privatized firms can be expected to undertake considerable fixed investment over the next few years.

We have not been able to identify a consistent breakdown by sector for the whole period but, according to InvestBulgaria statistics, 55 percent of FDI by the end of 1999 was in industry (around $1.55 billion); 19 percent ($543 million) in trade; and 11.5 percent ($324 million) in finance. In 2004 86 percent of FDI inflows went to the services sector, and 11 percent went to the manufacturing sector. Austria was the largest foreign investor between 1992 and June 2005, with $1.86 billion, followed by Greece ($1.09 billion), Germany ($916.2 million), and the Netherlands ($912.1 million).

The year 2001 was a relatively disappointing year for FDI in Bulgaria. Inward FDI dropped from a little over $1 billion in 2000 to $812.9 million in 2001. FDI inflows in 2001 were depressed by delays in privatization deals and they fell in the first quarter of 2002, to $46.8 million from $279.5 million a year earlier. A blow to hopes of attracting increased FDI was delivered when British American Tobacco, the world's second-largest cigarette firm, announced that it would close its Bulgarian subsidiary, having decided not to take part in the planned and subsequently abandoned sale of the state-owned Bulgartabak. FDI inflows did rebound, however, later in 2002, and 2003 was more promising. Inward FDI increased from a little over $900 million in 2002 to $2.1 billion in 2003. FDI inflows for 2004, at nearly $2.5 billion, were even more impressive. The 2004 levels were boosted by privatizations in the energy and telecommunications sectors.

Table 3. Foreign direct investment inflows, in $ million

	Privatization	Non-privatization	Total
1992		34.4	34.4
1993	22.0	80.4	102.4
1994	134.2	76.7	210.9
1995	26.0	136.6	162.6
1996	76.4	180.0	256.4
1997	421.4	214.8	636.2
1998	215.6	404.4	620.0
1999	226.7	592.1	818.8
2000	366.0	635.5	1,001.5
2001	19.2	793.7	812.9
2002	135.6	769.1	904.7
2003	353.5	1743.4	2096.9
2004	1189.7	1297.8	2487.5
Jan-June 2005	0.0	929.3	929.3
Total	*3186.3*	*7888.2*	*11074.5*

Source: InvestBulgaria Agency. Non-privatization: greenfield investment, additional investment in companies with foreign participation, reinvestment, joint ventures

The young, Western-educated former bankers who have run the economy since July 2001 have been pursuing market-friendly reforms, at the expense of some popular discontent, to win investor favor and impress NATO and the EU. Their reform efforts yielded a series of rating upgrades, a $300 million loan deal with the IMF in February 2002, a successful €250 million debut Eurobond issue in November 2001, and a swap of $1.33 billion Brady bonds into new fixed-rate global bonds in 2002. Furthermore, FDI has picked up since 2002.

The rest of this paper looks at medium-term prospects for FDI, utilizing a model that links FDI to measurements of the quality of a country's business environment.

FDI Determinants

Microeconomic and sectoral econometric studies, survey data, and aggregate econometric analysis have all been used in a growing body of empirical studies on the determinants and motives for FDI. According to the well-known theory elaborated by John Dunning (1993), FDI takes place when three sets of factors exist simultaneously: the presence of ownership-specific advantages in the investing multinational enterprise (MNE); the presence of locational advantages in a host country; and the existence of superior commercial benefits in an intra-firm transaction compared with the arm's-length relationship between investor and recipient. The ownership-specific advantages (proprietary technology) can compensate for the additional costs of establishing a firm in a foreign environment and the disadvantages compared with local firms. The firm benefits from "internalization" through FDI rather than arm's-length transactions. Only the second of these factors relates to host-country location factors, while the other two deal with the nature of the investing enterprise.

In an earlier book, Dunning (1981) provided an "eclectic" theory of the geographic distribution of FDI based on a series of location factors – including the availability of raw materials, labor costs, market characteristics, and government incentives. On the basis of the general theory and a large body of empirical literature, as well as inferences based on recent FDI experience, the following groups of potential FDI determinants can be identified. In general, empirical findings have demonstrated that FDI to the transition region is determined by similar factors as FDI to any other area.

Market size and growth. The drive to gain better market access has traditionally been the main determinant of most FDI activity, and this has tended to be confirmed by most empirical studies (with the market being measured by total GDP, GDP per head, and/or growth of GDP). Most empirical studies have confirmed this, and Eastern Europe is no exception. A survey of empirical studies on FDI in the region (Holland et al. 2000) found that most surveys of investors in the region and econometric evidence point to national and regional market access as the main factors influencing investors.

"Efficiency-seeking" investment. FDI takes place when expected risk-adjusted returns exceed costs by a margin that is greater than that which can be attained from alternative uses of funds. Therefore all investment (including that in search of market access) is in this sense "efficiency seeking." That is, it is affected by expected profitability, which will be higher the lower the cost of inputs. In the FDI literature, however, the term "efficiency seeking" has been reserved for investment that is primarily export oriented, which is especially sensitive to the costs of production and insensitive to the characteristics of the host-country market. Traditionally, the most important input costs have been those of labor. Wage costs are still important as an overall determinant of FDI activity, despite their low share in total costs in an increasing number of modern industries.

Survey evidence suggests that market size and growth potential have been the driving force behind investment in Eastern Europe, with factor cost advantages playing a lesser role. Econometric evidence especially for more recent periods does find that labor costs do play a role. Labor costs relative to other transition economies are more important than costs relative to other low-cost locations in the EU, such as Spain and Portugal. This may suggest a two-stage investment decision, where the investor first chooses to locate in Eastern Europe, and then chooses a location within the region (Holland and Pain 1998).

Geography and natural resources. The quest for natural resources has historically been one of the main motives for much FDI, especially in the developing world, although its relative importance has declined in parallel with the secular fall in the share of primary production in world output. Geography matters in other ways. Distances between home and host countries can still be important, despite the fact that technological change and the decline in transport and communication costs have reduced the impact of distance. Geographic location also impinges on the quest for better market access, insofar as FDI location decisions are based on efforts to gain access not only to national markets but also to wider regional markets. Geographic proximity also tends to be associated with cultural proximity. Many disadvantages of a host country as an investment destination can still be offset if that country has the same language and culture as the investor's home country.

A number of studies on Eastern Europe identify geographic factors such as distance as being significant, although results are often weak and not robust. This may not be surprising given that theory suggests that FDI replaces trade when large distances hinder trade, pointing to a possibly positive relationship between distance and FDI.

Agglomeration effects. There is evidence that FDI is spatially more clustered than other forms of production. Several mechanisms seem to be at work. Clustering of FDI may be attributable to positive linkages between projects, which create incentives to locate close to other firms. Investment around industry clusters allows savings to be made in transport costs and offers ready access to common input supplies and a large pool of skilled labor. A foreign investment presence can induce other foreign investments in the vertical chain, for example in suppliers or business service providers. The location of R&D activity can have a spillover effect, and there is also the possibility that firms "herd." Firms are uncertain whether a country is a good location, and they take the presence of other foreign firms as a positive and encouraging sign. Therefore, FDI can, to a certain extent, be self-perpetuating: competitors follow each other into a market.

The policy framework. Potential investment returns and costs, which form a country's overall business environment, are affected by a wide range of policies. The enabling framework for FDI – captured by the policy toward foreign investment in the EIU's business environment model (see appendix 2, "The Economist Intelligence Unit Business Environment Model") – consists of the rules and regulations governing the entry and operation of FDI. Although open FDI policies are a necessary condition, they are not a sufficient condition to attract FDI. A wide range of other policies (whether motivated by the desire to attract FDI or not) can influence FDI decisions. These are captured in the other categories of the EIU's business environment rankings (BER) model, and include government measures that influence institutional effectiveness, infrastructure and skill endowments, and macroeconomic and political stability. They also involve policies toward private enterprise in general: tax, labor market, financial sector, foreign trade, and exchange rate policies.

The existing empirical literature has estimated the effect of institutional development on FDI in the transition economies using indexes such as the European Bank of Reconstruction and Development (EBRD) index of reform progress (Bevan, Estrin, and Meyer 2000) or indexes of operational risk (Resmini 2000). A recent IMF study also found a significant influence on FDI of several institutional measures (Garibaldi et al. 2002). Institutions may be a particularly important determinant of FDI inflows in transition economies. Western businesses entering the transition economies face transaction costs that are higher than in mature market economies with developed institutional frameworks. Foreign entrants lack information about their partners and face unclear regulatory frameworks, an inexperienced bureaucracy, an underdeveloped court system, and corruption. All of this increases their search, negotiation, and enforcement costs (Bevan, Estrin, and Meyer 2000).

Empirical Estimation

The table below shows the results of a statistical exercise where the logs of average FDI inflows in 1996-2000 into the twenty-seven Eastern European countries were related to a number of variables that influence FDI. The exercise looked at dollar GDP, dollar wages, the EIU's business environment index, a measure of natural resource endowments, and a privatization index. The latter variable is an index (taking values of 0, 1 and 2), which is similar to indexes already used in the literature (Holland and Pain 1998), which measure the ability and readiness of authorities to sell assets to foreign-

Table 4. Estimating FDI inflows, 1996-2000

	Coefficients	t Stat	Coefficients	t Stat	Coefficients	t Stat	Coefficients	t Stat
Constant	-3.382	-11.167	-3.038	-8.752	-2.993	-7.262	-3.351	-9.499
Log GDP	0.836	27.254	0.818	26.574	0.826	26.809	0.834	24.519
BE adj	0.258	5.508	0.199	3.562	0.169	3.127	0.255	5.094
Oil dummy	0.244	1.916	0.299	2.398	0.255	2.044	0.248	1.874
Azerbaijan	1.683	7.368	1.679	7.732	1.732	7.645	1.680	7.151
Wages	-0.173	-3.683	-0.167	-3.725	-0.164	-3.527	-0.175	-3.549
Priv	0.494	8.896	0.493	9.342	0.527	8.837	0.494	8.675
EU 1			0.218	1.774				
EU 2					0.239	1.362		
EU 3							0.025	0.185
Adjusted R2	0.983		0.985		0.983		0.982	

GDP - $million 1996-2000 average

BE adj - Business environments score adjusted to exclude market opportunities

Oil dummy - Variable taking value 1 for oil producers

Azerbaijan - Dummy variable for Azerbaijan

Wages - Monthly dollar wages 1998-99

Priv - Index of privatization method; see text

EU 1 - Dummy variable taking the value of 1 for the 10 EU associate countries (Bulgaria, Czech Republic, Estonia, Hungary, Latvia, Lithuania, Poland, Romania, Slovakia, Slovenia)

EU 2 - Dummy variable taking the value of 1 for eight EU associate countries likely to be included in the first round of EU enlargement: all except Bulgaria and Romania

ers. Ability in the period in question will be impaired if, as in Hungary and Estonia, most assets have already been sold. The readiness is assessed on the basis of information reported by the EBRD on the privatization receipts as a percentage of GDP and on the primary method adopted in each country for privatization.

The estimation was very satisfactory, with almost the entire inter-country variation in FDI flows in 1996-2000 being explained by the variables in our parsimonious specification. As expected, market size was one of the most significant variables. The coefficients of determination were unusually high. There was one "outlier" country, Azerbaijan, either because the natural resource variable we use is too crude or, more significantly, because there is every indication that Azerbaijan's dollar GDP is even more underestimated than is usual in these economies (with Azerbaijan in the sample the R2 declines by a couple of points). The set of variables generated reasonable estimates for all the other countries in the sample (table 5).

The results suggest that FDI inflows are very sensitive to the policy framework. The business environment index was highly significant and robust to alternative speci-

Table 5. Predicted and actual FDI

FDI 1996–2000 average $ million			FDI 1996–2000 average $ million		
	Predicted	Actual		Predicted	Actual
Czech Republic	3,141	3,463	Russia	4,182	3,246
Hungary	1,776	2,020	Ukraine	534	596
Poland	6,664	6,477	Belarus	246	239
Slovakia	732	699	Moldova	77	70
Slovenia	264	235	Armenia	153	103
Albania	74	73	Azerbaijan	na	na
Bosnia and Herzegovina	79	78	Georgia	182	152
Bulgaria	**585**	**594**	Kazakhstan	1,269	1,289
Croatia	791	914	Kyrgyz Republic	41	56
Macedonia	91	70	Tajikistan	25	24
Romania	932	1,115	Turkmenistan	74	100
Yugoslavia	197	226	Uzbekistan	149	119
Estonia	322	338			
Latvia	315	403			
Lithuania	460	460			

fications. The findings tend to be confirmed by the results of most business surveys, which continue to highlight market access as still having a major influence on location decisions. The results show that wage costs are a significant factor for FDI. The natural resource variables are also found to be significant, although less so, and are less robust than other variables in the model (but this may be the result of shortcomings in the exercise's measurement of natural resources). The privatization variable is also highly significant. Alternative measures of natural resources were also used (share of exports accounted for by fuel and metals), but the results were not materially affected. The impact of distance was also tested (distance between the capital city and Dusseldorf), but no significant impact could be identified. Education levels were tested; again this variable proved insignificant. Thus our results show that market size (measured by dollar GDP), the quality of the overall business environment, wage costs, natural resource endowments, and privatization methods statistically explain almost the entire inter-country variation in FDI receipts in the region in 1996-2000.

Finally we tested for another standard assumption, that EU accession expectations affect FDI. Interestingly the more obvious definitions of the EU factor (which exclude Bulgaria and Romania) had a very weak, statistically insignificant effect. This means that although it is possible for the EU factor, in terms of accession prospects, to affect business environments, no independent effect over and above that could be identified. Only when Bulgaria and Romania were included in the definition of the EU variable did the estimated coefficient approach significance. This strongly suggests that what is being measured is market access to the EU, rather than accession prospects (otherwise the other two EU dummy variables would have performed better), which all ten applicant countries enjoyed. It is market access that appears to be crucial for FDI, and this is not the same as accession-related expectations.

FDI and EU Accession

There is a widespread expectation that EU accession, by reducing risk and transaction costs, will be accompanied by an increase in foreign investment. EU entry is expected to make the East European countries more attractive as a production location for multinational companies because it will guarantee free access to a market with around 480 million consumers (Kaminski 2001; Brenton, di Mauro, and Lucke 1998). Enlargement is expected to remove most hurdles for cross-border economic transactions and insure investors against sudden changes in trade policy. Furthermore, the process of preparing for accession itself promotes higher FDI. The adoption of EU rules and regulations helps create a business environment similar to that in Western European countries. It reduces the risk of arbitrary policy changes in the East, for example in indirect taxation; makes property rights even more secure; and is likely to enhance political stability (for example, Baldwin, Francois, and Portes 1997). In a simple econometric exercise, which was probably affected by an omitted variable bias (for example, market size and other relevant variables were not controlled for), Oleh Havrylyshyn (1998) found that being a potential EU accession country was positively associated with FDI receipts.

Bevan and Estrin (2000) report econometric evidence that expectations of EU accession have affected FDI into the region. They look at the public commitment made by EU member states on enlarging eastwards. Having controlled for other factors that affect FDI, they find that the 1994 Essen Council announcement was associated with a significant increase in the level of FDI received by the frontrunner countries for EU accession – the Czech Republic, Hungary, and Poland. The Agenda 2000 announcement is found to have led to an increase in the growth rate of FDI to the first-wave applicants. FDI may be further affected if perceptions about EU accession negatively affect institutional reform (which also attracts FDI) because of a loss of popular support for reform in the applicant countries furthest from membership. FDI inflows would thus, according to this reasoning, look likely to become increasingly concentrated in the frontrunners, as EU decisions reinforce investors' preferences. This process would thus result in a widening of differences in economic performance in the region. The gap in regional growth and development will thus potentially widen rather than narrow (Bevan, Estrin, and Grabbe 2001). Another important implication is that further delays to enlargement would cause FDI inflows into the leading applicant countries to drop. If it becomes clear that countries are not going to join the EU for many years, businesses will then alter their strategies for pan-European markets and FDI inflows will drop off, holding back economic integration and progress in transition as well. Several reasons exist for being skeptical about the proposition that EU accession expectations among investors have a decisive influence on FDI:

- The EU anchor may not be crucial for further improvements in business environments as long as political democracy is established. Strong evidence was found that the latter is the main determinant of changes in the quality of the business environment (Kekic 2001).
- Some EU-related polices are inimical to growth and FDI.
- The experience of the relationship between FDI and earlier enlargements is mixed.
- The exercise's statistical analysis does not support the view that there is an independent effect of the EU accession factor, once other FDI determinants, including the quality of the business environment, have been controlled for.

Many of the individual institutional reforms required for EU accession have undoubtedly positively influenced the business environment and thus FDI inflows. However, some reforms may even work to reduce FDI inflows. Many EU reforms are detrimental to growth and the quality of the business environment. Harmonization imposes hefty spending requirements that are not met by EU transfers in the pre-accession phase. The pursuit of nominal macroeconomic convergence may be at the expense of growth that attracts FDI. The adoption of many costly EU standards is not appropriate to transition economies' level of development and may also hinder growth.

Previous rounds of EU enlargement provide mixed evidence on the relationship between accession and FDI. In both Portugal and Spain, risk premiums declined with EU entry and there was a sharp increase in FDI compared with very low levels in the period preceding membership. However, the case of Greece shows that the benefits from EU membership do not come automatically. Because of the country's misguided economic policies and continued political uncertainty, Greece's EU entry did not make a difference in its paltry FDI inflows. Between 1981 and 1999 annual FDI inflows into Greece averaged, with remarkably little inter-year variation, a very modest 1.2 percent of GDP per year. In Austria, too, the stock of FDI rose only relatively modestly after EU accession, from 6.2 percent of GDP in 1990 to 8.6 percent in 1997. As for Spain and Portugal, despite better policies than in Greece, a more favorable business environment, and a strong FDI response in the period immediately following EU accession, the long-term record of these two countries initially did not seem to be that much more favorable: FDI inflows in 1987-99 averaged 2 percent per year in Portugal and 1.8 percent in Spain. However, these figures did improve during 2001-04, with FDI inflows to Spain and Portugal in this period reaching 3.4 percent and 2.9 percent respectively.

Political economy considerations do suggest that the expectation of EU accession and most associated policy requirements have provided an anchor for the pursuit of reforms that enhance the quality of the overall business environment. However, provided that market access can be secured through trade liberalization, no evidence was found of any further independent impact on FDI of the EU accession factor. The findings suggest that transition countries that can improve their business environments gain access to EU markets and those that have privatization programs encouraging foreign sales can attract significant volumes of FDI, irrespective of geographic factors and the lack of EU accession prospects.

Forecasting Bulgarian FDI for 2001-05

Expected improvements in the business environment underpinned the expectation of relatively buoyant FDI in Bulgaria over the 2001-05 period. Utilizing the model of FDI determination explained above, Bulgaria's FDI over the 2001-05 period is forecast to average about $900 million per year. For the 2001-04 period, actual FDI averaged nearly $1.6 billion. The assumptions that supported these projections were that 1) real GDP would grow by about 4 percent to 4.5 percent per year, which combined with appreciation against the U.S. dollar would boost dollar GDP at a rate of about 10 percent per year; 2) average dollar wages were also expected to grow by 10 percent per year; 3) privatization policy would focus on strategic sales; and 4) above all, there would be a considerable improvement in the overall business environment. Bulgaria's better business environment in 2001-05 than in the previous five years of 1996-2000 is reflected in a jump of seven places in the EIU's business environment rankings.

Select Medium-term Trends in the Bulgarian Business Environment

Beginning with the political environment, following is a brief examination of various factors that can be expected to influence the business environment in Bulgaria.

Political Environment

Risks to political stability are relatively low. Democracy is firmly established, as are smooth transitions from one government to another. The former government was not able to fulfill voters' high expectations, which led to greater support for the center-left opposition and the latter's return to power following the mid-2005 elections.

Table 6. Business environment scores and ranks

| | 2001–05 | | 1996–2000 | | 2001–05/1996–2000 | |
	Total Score	Regional Rank	Total Score	Regional Rank	Δ Score	Δ Rank
Estonia	7.4	1	6.86	1	0.54	0
Hungary	7.26	2	6.42	2	0.83	0
Poland	7.07	3	6.22	3	0.85	0
Czech Republic	7.01	4	6.18	4	0.83	0
Slovenia	6.96	5	6.08	5	0.87	0
Lithuania	6.95	6	5.74	7	1.21	1
Latvia	6.88	7	5.87	6	1.01	-1
Slovakia	6.57	8	5.46	8	1.11	0
Croatia	6.33	9	5.23	9	1.1	0
Bulgaria	*5.94*	*10*	*4.03*	*17*	*1.91*	*7*
Kazakhstan	5.59	11	4.3	13	1.29	2
Russia	5.49	12	4.12	14	1.36	2
Armenia	5.34	13	4.5	10	0.84	-3
Azerbaijan	5.28	14	4.35	12	0.92	-2
Romania	5.24	15	4.1	15	1.14	0
Yugoslavia	5.23	16	2.79	27	2.44	11
Macedonia	5.21	17	4.47	11	0.73	-6
Albania	5.09	18	4.01	19	1.07	1
Ukraine	4.95	19	3.27	23	1.69	4
Georgia	4.87	20	4.01	18	0.86	-2
Moldova	4.78	21	4.04	16	0.74	-5
Kyrgyz Republic	4.77	22	3.75	22	1.02	0
Bosnia and Herzegovina	4.66	23	3.98	20	0.68	-3
Belarus	4.16	24	3.91	21	0.25	-3
Tajikistan	3.55	25	2.81	25	0.74	0
Turkmenistan	3.46	26	3.05	24	0.41	-2
Uzbekistan	3.18	27	2.8	26	0.38	-1

The former government, which came to power partly on the strength of public disillusionment with corruption, did improve the effectiveness of the judicial system somewhat. This will benefit businesses, for example, by reducing the scope for unfair business practices and increasing the opportunities for legal remedies. One business risk arising from the anticorruption drive is that bureaucrats may not use their initiative for fear that flexibility will be seen as corruption. Despite the inherent difficulties of anticorruption measures, and difficulties in recruiting and retaining skilled staff, public administration should become more efficient over the medium term.

Macroeconomic Stability

The currency board system will continue to be the basis for macroeconomic stability. As Bulgaria's currency is linked to that of its main trading partner, the euro zone, Bulgaria's currency board should be less vulnerable than Argentina's proved to be. After the successful completion of a three-year agreement for an SDR 627.6 million ($850 million) extended fund facility (EFF) with the IMF, which expired in 2001, Bulgaria signed an SDR 240 million ($299 million) two-year standby agreement with the IMF in February 2002. In August 2004, the IMF approved a new two-year standby agreement for SDR 100 million ($146 million) to support the government's economic program for 2004-06.

The World Bank's structural adjustment and investment programs for Bulgaria during the 2002-05 period are expected to total $750 million. In December 2002, the bank approved a $50 million loan for a social investment and employment promotion project (SIEP) to improve the standard of living and employment prospects for people residing in pockets of poverty in Bulgaria. The bank also approved a $150 million programmatic adjustment loan (PAL) for Bulgaria in February 2003 and in June 2004. PAL 1 supported improvements in the business environment, the restructuring of infrastructure sectors, and the further deepening of the financial sector. PAL 2 continues the reforms initiated under PAL 1 and also supports efforts to improve public sector governance.

Policy toward Foreign Investment

The previous government created a more efficient and investor-friendly apparatus for promoting foreign investment, and the present government is likely to build on this. Rules governing the ownership of nonagricultural land by partly foreign-owned companies have been relaxed and the government has indicated that it wants to relax them further. The ban on foreign ownership of agricultural land may take longer to be lifted. Specific tax breaks for foreign investors were phased out in 1997. Government officials have talked of introducing special incentives, but the hostility of the EU and the IMF makes a general scheme of incentives for foreign investors unlikely. Some incentives for all investors in depressed areas may be permitted, although more generalized tax breaks – the subject of a past dispute with the IMF – were initially ruled out based on fiscal concerns.

Foreign Exchange Regime

Tariff cuts were instituted at the beginning of 1999 and were an obligation arising from Bulgaria's membership in the World Trade Organization (WTO). Liberalization has continued since, with the abolition of some registration requirements and of fees levied on exports of certain types of raw materials. The review of licensing and registration requirements will further reduce restrictions on foreign trade. Additional impetus for trade liberalization has come from numerous free-trade agreements signed in recent years, including the country's association agreement with the EU and membership in the Central European Free-Trade Agreement (CEFTA), which came into force at the beginning of 1999.

Tax Regime

Until fairly recently Bulgaria had one of the world's more illiberal tax systems, with high corporate tax rates, restrictive definitions of allowable business expenses, and poorly drafted rules that gave tax officials wide scope for arbitrary interpretation. Improvements are expected over the medium term. The Tax Procedures Code passed in late 1999 was an important step toward creating a more stable environment, although businesses are likely to find that changes are still too frequent for comfort. Tax rules will remain fairly restrictive over the next few years because of the government's revenue requirements. A crackdown on evasion, coupled with steady improvements in public administration and technology, should reduce favoritism toward politically well-connected businesses.

The resultant broadening of the revenue base is allowing direct tax rates to be reduced. The standard rate of corporate profit tax payable to the central government was cut from 25 percent at the start of 2000 to a uniform rate of 15 percent at the start of 2002. This figure represents an overall profit tax rate of 23.5 percent, because 10 percent of what remains after central government profit tax has been deducted is still payable as municipal profit tax. An election promise of zero corporate tax on reinvested profits was delayed because of objections from the IMF, and political pressures mean that progress toward this objective is likely to be slow. However, aggregate taxes on corporate profits were cut to 19.5 percent in 2004 and will be cut again in 2005 to 15 percent, freeing an estimated LV250 million for the private sector.

Financial Sector

Improvements in the banking sector are expected to continue. Much of this improvement will be the result of the high level of foreign ownership. From 1997 to 2003, the state sold United Bulgarian Bank, the Bulgarian Post Bank, Hebros Bank, Bulbank, Biochim, and DSK Bank. Bulbank – the system's largest bank – was privatized in the second half of 2000. Biochim Bank was sold to Bank Austria Creditanstalt Group in July 2002, and the privatization of DSK Bank was completed in October 2003. Lending volumes for both companies and households have been growing quite quickly since 2000. The availability of funds from a variety of foreign and multilateral sources will remove some constraints on commercial lending.

Labor Market

A skilled and literate workforce, weak trade unions, and relatively low U.S. dollar wages have made the labor market one of the strongest features of Bulgaria's business environment, and further improvements are expected. However, as seems to be a common problem across Eastern Europe, the cumulative effects of low spending could reduce the quality of the education system. Another problem is that although emigration will be low in absolute terms, those moving abroad will continue to be disproportionately drawn from the pool of highly skilled workers.

Infrastructure

More improvements to the telecom sector will lead to an increase in overall line density as the program to shift to a digital fixed-line network gathers momentum. The pace of development was spurred both by the much-delayed privatization of the public telecom operator, BTC, in June 2004, and by the expiration of BTC's fixed-line monopoly at the end of 2002, which have allowed competition to raise standards.

The authorities will focus on integrating Bulgaria's transport system into European and intercontinental networks. Investment will be concentrated on EU-aided road repair schemes; extensions to motorways; the modernization of the state railways, including construction of a high-speed link with Thessalonica in Greece; and the modernization of the port at Burgas. Energy policy will be dominated by the separation of the production and distribution of electricity. In November 2003 Bulgaria adopted a new energy law that set the framework for the gradual opening up of its gas and electricity sectors.

Appendix 1: Bulgaria business environment rankings

	Value of index (out of 10)		Regional rank (out of 27)	
	1996-2000	*2001-05*	*1996-2000*	*2001-05*
Overall scores and ranks	**4.03**	**5.94**	**17**	**10**
Political environment	4.1	5.7	11	9
Political stability	5.0	6.8	10	9
Political effectiveness	3.3	4.8	12	10
Macroeconomic environment	3.0	7.5	22	9
Market opportunities	1.3	3.7	26	20
Policy toward private enterprise and competition	3.8	6.1	13	10
Policy toward foreign investment	5.5	6.6	8	9
Foreign trade and exchange controls	4.9	7.2	16	11
Taxes	3.9	5.6	17	11
Financing	2.9	4.8	13	12
Labor market	5.6	6.3	23	17
Infrastructure	5.3	6.0	7	7

Appendix 2: EIU Business Environment Model

The Economist Intelligence Unit's business rankings model measures the quality or attractiveness of the business environment. It is designed to reflect the main criteria used by companies to formulate their global business strategies, and is based not only on historical conditions but also on expectations about conditions prevailing over the next five years. The business rankings model examines ten separate criteria or categories, covering the political environment, the macroeconomic environment, market opportunities, policy toward free enterprise and competition, policy toward foreign investment, foreign trade and exchange controls, taxes, financing, the labor market, and infrastructure. Each category contains a number of indicators that are assessed by the EIU for the last five years and the next five years. There are seventy indicators in total.

Almost half of the indicators are based on quantitative data (for example, GDP growth), and are mostly drawn from national and international statistical sources (see sources below) for the historical period (1996-2000). Scores for the forecast period (2001-05) are based on EIU forecasts. The other indicators are qualitative in nature (for example, quality of the financial regulatory system) and are drawn from a range of data sources and business surveys, frequently adjusted by the EIU, for 1996-2000. All forecasts for the qualitative indicators covering 2001-05 are based on EIU assessments.

Calculating the Rankings

The rankings are calculated in several stages. First, each of the seventy indicators is scored on a scale from 1 (very bad for business) to 5 (very good for business). The aggregate category scores are derived on the basis of simple or weighted averages of the indicator scores within a given category. These are then adjusted, on the basis of a linear transformation, to produce index values on a 1-10 scale. An arithmetic average of the ten-category index values is then calculated to yield the aggregate business environment score for each country, again on a 1-10 scale.

The use of equal weights for the categories to derive the overall score reflects in part the theoretical uncertainty about the relative importance of the primary determinants of investment. Surveys of foreign direct investors' intentions yield widely differing results on the relative importance of different factors. Weighted scores for individual categories based on correlation coefficients of recent foreign direct investment inflows do not in any case produce overall results that are significantly different from those derived from a system based on equal weights. For most quantitative indicators the data are arrayed in ascending or descending order and split into five bands (quintiles). The countries falling in the first quintile are assigned scores of 5, those falling in the second quintile score 4, and so on. The cutoff points between bands are based on the average of the raw indicator values for the top and bottom countries in adjacent quintiles. The 1996-2000 ranges are then used to derive 2001-05 scores. This allows for inter-temporal as well as cross-country comparisons of the indicator and category scores.

Figure 1. Summary indicators in the business rankings model

Political Environment
1. Risk of armed conflict
2. Risk of social unrest
3. Constitutional mechanisms for the orderly transfer of power
4. Threat of politically motivated violence
5. International disputes or tensions
6. Government policy toward business
7. Effectiveness of political system in policy formulation and execution
8. Quality of the bureaucracy
9. Transparency and fairness of political system
10. Corruption
11. Impact of crime

Macroeconomic Environment
*1. Inflation
*2. Budget balance as percent of GDP
*3. Government debt as percent of GDP
*4. Exchange-rate volatility
*5. Current-account balance as percent of GDP

Market Opportunities
*1. GDP, $ billion at PPP
*2. GDP per head, $ at PPP
*3. Real GDP growth
*4. Share of world merchandise trade
*5. Average annual rate of growth of exports
*6. Average annual rate of growth of imports
*7. The natural resource endowment
*8. Profitability

Policy toward Private Enterprise and Competition
1. Degree to which private property rights are protected
2. Government regulation on setting up new private businesses
3. Freedom of existing businesses to compete
4. Promotion of competition
5. Protection of intellectual property
6. Price controls
7. Distortions arising from lobbying by special interest groups
8. Distortions arising from state ownership/control

Policy toward Foreign Investment
1. Government policy toward foreign capital
2. Openness of national culture to foreign influences
3. Risk of expropriation of foreign assets
4. Availability of investment protection schemes

Foreign Trade and Exchange Controls
1. Capital-account liberalization
**2. Tariff and non-tariff protection
*3. Openness of trade
4. Restrictions on the current account

Taxes
**1. Corporate tax burden
*2. Top marginal personal income tax
*3. Value-added tax
*4. Employers' social security contributions
5. Degree to which fiscal regime encourages new investment
6. Consistency and fairness of the tax system

Financing
1. Openness of banking sector
2. Stock market capitalization
**3. Distortions in financial markets
4. Quality of the financial regulatory system
5. Access by foreigners to local capital market
6. Access to medium-term financing for investment

Labor Market
**1. Incidence of strikes
*2. Labor costs adjusted for productivity
*3. Availability of skilled labor
4. Quality of workforce
5. Restrictiveness of labor laws
6. Extent of wage regulation
7. Hiring of foreign nationals
*8. Cost of living

Infrastructure
*1. Telephone density
**2. Reliability of telecoms network
**3. Extent and quality of road network
*4. Production of electricity per head
**5. The infrastructure for retail and wholesale distribution
**6. Extent and quality of the rail network
7. Quality of ports infrastructure
*8. Stock of personal computers
*9. R&D expenditure as percent of GDP
*10. Rents of office space

Note: A single asterisk (*) denotes a purely quantitative indicator. Indicators with a double asterisk (**) are partly based on data. All other indicators are qualitative in nature.

Weights

The overall business environment score is derived as an unweighted average of the ten category scores. Alternative weights based on the correlation coefficients of FDI inflows in 1996-99 with the individual category scores did not yield markedly different results. The use of average business survey results (which tend to vary widely) yielded similar rankings to the equal-weight method. The use of equal weights is in part a reflection of ignorance about the relative importance of various determinants of business decisions. It may be supported by empirical findings on the importance of policy complementarities, which suggest that economic performance depends on good policies being applied across the board, that is, very good polices in one area cannot offset poor policies in another. The equal-weight method is likely to be a closer reflection of the latter point than a weighting system that assigned above-average significance to some categories.

References

Baldwin, Richard, Jean Francois, and Richard Portes. 1997. The costs and benefits of eastern enlargement: The impact on the EU and Central Europe. *Economic Policy* 24 (April).

Bevan, Alan, Saul Estrin, and Klaus Meyer. 2000. Institution building and the integration of Eastern Europe in international production. Centre for New and Emerging Markets Discussion Paper Series, no. 11 (December), London Business School.

Bevan, Alan, and Saul Estrin. 2000. The determinants of foreign direct investment in transition economies. CEPR Discussion Paper 2638 (December), Centre for Economic Policy Research, London.

Bevan, Alan, Saul Estrin, and Heather Grabbe. 2001. The impact of EU accession prospects on FDI inflows to Central and Eastern Europe. Policy paper (June). Centre for New and Emerging Markets, London Business School, and Centre for European Reform, London.

Borensztein, Eduardo, Jose De Gregorio, and Jong-Wha Lee. 1998. How does foreign direct investment affect growth? *Journal of International Economics* 45, no. 1.

Brenton, Paul, Francesca di Mauro, and Matthias Lucke. 1998. Economic integration and FDI: an empirical analysis of foreign investment in the EU and Eastern Europe. CEPS Working Paper 124 (November). Brussels.

Dunning, John. 1993. *Multinational enterprises and the global economy.* Wokingham: Addison-Wesley.

Dunning, John. 1981. *International production and the multinational enterprise.* London: Allen and Unwin.

EBRD. 2000. *Transition report 2000: Employment, skills and transition.* London: EBRD.

Economist Intelligence Unit. 2001. East European investment prospects. London.

Economist Intelligence Unit. 2002. *Country report: Bulgaria* (May).

Economist Intelligence Unit. 2005. *Country report: Bulgaria* (October).

Garibaldi, Pietro, Nada Mora, Ratna Sahaya, and Jeromin Zettelmeyer. 2002. What moves capital to transition economies? IMF Working Paper WP/02/64.

Havrylyshyn, Oleh. 1998. EU enlargement and possible echoes beyond the new frontiers. Paper presented at the Vienna Institute for International Economic Studies twenty-fifth anniversary conference (November), Vienna.

Holland, Dawn, and Nigel Pain. 1998. The diffusion of innovations in Central and Eastern Europe: a study of the determinants and impact of foreign direct investment. Discussion Paper 137, National Institute of Economic and Social Research, London.

Holland, Dawn, Magdolna Sass, Vladimir Benacek, and Miroslaw Gronicki. 2000. The determinants and impact of FDI in Central and Eastern Europe: A comparison of survey and econometric evidence. *Transnational Corporations* 9, no. 3 (December).

Kaminski, Bartlomiej. 2001. How accession to the European Union has affected external trade and foreign direct investment in Central European economies. World Bank Policy Research Working Paper 2578.

Kekic, Laza. 2001. Foreign direct investment in Eastern Europe: Trends and forecasts. Economist Intelligence Unit.

Resmini, Laura, The determinants of foreign direct investment in the CEECs. *Economics of Transition* 8, no. 3.

UN Conference on Trade and Development. 2001. *World investment report 2001*. New York: UNCTAD.

UN Economic Commission for Europe. 2001. Economic growth and foreign direct investment in transition economies. *Economic Survey of Europe*, no. 1 (May).

6 Economic Reform in Bulgaria: Main Achievements and Challenges

By Martin Hallet, Economist, Directorate-General for Economic and Financial Affairs, European Commission

Edited and updated paper based on the conference as submitted in April 2003[1]

In its 2002 Regular Report on Bulgaria's progress toward accession, the European Commission concluded in its assessment on the economic accession criteria that "Bulgaria is a functioning market economy. It should be able to cope with competitive pressure and market forces within the Union in the medium term, provided that it continues implementing its reform programme to remove remaining difficulties" (European Commission 2002). Given that in 2001 the commission had only concluded that Bulgaria is "close to being a functioning market economy" and that it should "intensify" the reform effort, credit was given to the progress made by 2002.

The economic reform process in Bulgaria is to a large extent driven by the preparation for EU accession. However, while fulfilling the criteria for EU membership is not a goal in itself, it will help to achieve the ultimate goal to increase citizens' living standards on a sustained basis, which is usually measured by income per capita. This paper proceeds by asking some basic questions on economic reforms. From this perspective, the state of play of economic reforms in Bulgaria will then be described, followed by concluding remarks.

Basic Aspects of Economic Reforms

Carrying out economic reforms is an extremely complex exercise, which involves political difficulties of equal complexity. Macroeconomic stabilization and structural reforms play out differently in different types of economies (such as industrialized, developing, and transition economies) in different parts of the world and historical periods, making almost each case unique. Nevertheless, by consulting the vast

---

1 The views expressed in this paper are exclusively those of the author and do not necessarily correspond to those of the European Commission, for whose Directorate-General for Economic and Financial Affairs the author is working. However, the discussion of the state of play ("Main Achievements and Challenges in Bulgaria") draws primarily from European Commission (2002) and therefore largely corresponds to the views of the European Commission.

amounts of literature that exist about the topic, it is possible to formulate answers to some general questions on economic reforms. In essence, economic reforms aiming at macroeconomic stability and flexible product, capital, and labor markets make it possible to achieve:

- Efficiency gains by improving the allocation of resources and reducing monopoly rents through lower price-cost margins. These static and dynamic efficiency gains provide producers with the right incentives for investment and production as well as providing consumers with lower prices and a better choice of product qualities.
- An efficient adjustment toward external and internal equilibriums in terms of the current account deficit, inflation, and unemployment. This is particularly important in fixed exchange rate regimes, such as a currency board arrangement, where the nominal exchange rate is not available for swift adjustment to a changing external environment. Structural reforms are also important for sound fiscal policies in transition periods when tax revenues are still low and privatization brings about revenues and a reduction of subsidies.

Economic reforms are not an objective by themselves nor are they carried out to please international organizations, but – like all good economic policies – they should improve the welfare in an economy on a sustained basis. However, economies undergoing drastic reforms usually have a j-shaped slope of production and income over time. In the short run, the reallocation of resources usually involves substantial adjustment costs in the form of income losses and higher unemployment. These are, however, outweighed by the medium- to long-term benefits, which provide higher income growth and new job opportunities compared to the no-reform scenario.

In view of the short-term costs of economic reforms, political stability is obviously an essential condition for their successful implementation. Therefore, both accompanying social policy measures and a good communication policy explaining to the public the need for – and the impact of – individual reform measures are important elements. While international organizations can be useful scapegoats for justifying unpopular reforms, this might not be sufficient as an exclusive justification since public opinion might eventually turn against these organizations and put the reform process at risk. It is essential to make citizens aware that most reforms cannot be avoided anyway and that their postponement will only increase the costs of their implementation.

The speed and sequencing of economic reforms have been a continuing subject of economic debate.[2] "Gradualism" and "shock therapy" are the keywords for the two opposite approaches, one advocating a slow implementation of reform programs,

---

2   For a recent summary of the discussion see Nsouli et al. (2002).

the other a fast implementation. The baseline of this debate is that it is impossible to draw general conclusions and that country-specific factors for a range of criteria, including the initial economic conditions and the political situation, need to be looked at. "As soon as possible" is therefore a rather vague but possibly still adequate answer to the question of speed, which acknowledges that certain reforms can be postponed for only a limited amount of time before a more severe economic crisis occurs. In regard to sequencing, there is some agreement that institutional reform and fiscal and monetary stabilization are priorities while the right time for the liberalization of the capital account continues to be debated.

The high priority for macroeconomic stabilization arises from, among other causes, the fact that high inflation rates do not allow prices to give the right signals to markets for the efficient allocation of resources. Equally, a continuously high budget deficit and the corresponding accumulation of debt divert the limited capital to the public sector that could often be more efficiently used in the private sector. Furthermore, this exerts a tendency to increase the current account deficit through a number of channels.

A basic requirement for a market economy is that private property rights be enforceable and that the transaction costs for exchanging goods be low. This will ensure that the owner alone decides on the use of a right, which will become the property of the person who values it most in terms of willingness to pay. This is why markets – depending on the size of transaction costs and the efficiency of regulation – have a tendency to allocate goods to their most valuable use through price mechanisms, which reveal the value of a property right. An important reform step in this respect is to improve the functioning of the administrative and judicial systems, including the fight against corruption, in order to ensure the rule of law. Price liberalization is also a basic requirement in order to allow prices to give the right signals to producers and consumers.

Given the high share of inefficient state-owned companies in central planning economies, their privatization usually goes along with substantial improvements in productivity and profitability, which are unavoidably accompanied by employment losses. While there are different views on the best ways of transferring firms from state ownership into private ownership, it is uncontroversial that privatization needs to be complemented by more competition in the respective sectors and the risk of failure in the form of bankruptcy by avoiding soft budget constraints through bail-outs from the government. Otherwise, there will be no gains or even losses from changing a state-owned monopoly into a private monopoly or from subsidizing loss-making private firms.

Improving the efficiency of regulation is important to facilitate the conditions for doing business. Strong reliance on large-scale production in socialist times basically implied the absence of small and medium-sized enterprises (SMEs) in socialist economies, making it all the more necessary to facilitate the startup of new firms. There are often too many licensing requirements for starting a new enterprise, which also increases the potential for corruption in the public service. Efficient regulation involves particular difficulties for utility networks; experiences in Germany (energy, rail), the United States (electricity), and the United Kingdom (rail) provide several examples of incomplete deregulation and liberalization. The problem is that the network infrastructure itself may require a high degree of regulation – or even continued state ownership – to allow the services transmitted via the infrastructure to develop a sufficient degree of competition.

External liberalization is another important reform element that brings about substantial gains from trade and capital flows. However, the adequate sequencing with other reform measures required for maintaining external competitiveness, in particular regarding the liberalization of capital movements, is a difficult task. Significant exchange rate misalignments, for example, can lead to major external imbalances in the case of a premature opening up of the economy.

Apart from economic reforms, a sustained process of income catch-up also requires efficient institutions, good infrastructure, and a skilled workforce. These aspects are the priorities of EU pre-accession instruments in candidate countries (PHARE, ISPA, SAPARD[3]) and of EU structural funds and the Cohesion Fund in member states.

Main Achievements and Challenges in Bulgaria

Bulgaria lost a lot of time in the early 1990s by postponing economic transition and only started implementing serious economic reforms after the economic and financial crisis of the winter 1996-97. Because of the overall bad economic performance in the 1990s culminating in the crisis, average GDP per capita (in purchasing power standards, or PPS) remained low in the late 1990s and 2001-02, at 26 percent to 28 percent of the EU average, and little progress was made in catching up to EU income levels. Figure 1 plots GDP per capita in PPS for the transition candidate countries relative to the fifteen EU countries (EU15) in 1995 against the change of this indicator in percentage points between 1995 and 2001. It can be seen that Bulgaria was among those countries whose relative income position declined compared to its 1995 level by about 5 percentage points, whereas other countries – where reforms started much

---

3   PHARE: Poland and Hungary Assistance for Economic Restructuring, a pre-accession instrument that originated in 1989 to support economic reconstruction in Poland and Hungary. Subsequently, the program has been extended to other countries of Central and Eastern Europe, and since 2000 it focuses on two priorities in the adoption of the acquis: institution building and investment support; ISPA: Instrument for Structural Policies for Pre-accession; SAPARD: Special Assistance Program for Agricultural and Rural Development.

earlier – have gained by up to 8.6 percentage points. In 2004, Bulgaria's GDP per PPS was approximately 30 percent of the enlarged EU.

Macroeconomic Stabilization

The currency board arrangement, which was introduced in July 1997 by fixing the Bulgarian lev against the euro, has contributed to containing inflation and to stabilizing the economy. Real GDP growth, which was minus 5.6 percent in 1997, was close to 4 percent on average since 1998 and consumer price inflation came down from 1,058 percent on average in 1997 to single-digit rates (see table 1). Macroeconomic stability and economic growth were sustained in spite of successive adverse external conditions, including the Kosovo crisis, the conflict in the former Yugoslav Republic of Macedonia, the economic crisis in Turkey, and the global economic slowdown. Real GDP growth in 2002 was 4.9 percent. It was largely based on buoyant domestic demand, in particular investment growth, while the external balance continues to be a drag on growth. In 2003, real GDP grew by 4.3 percent, and 2004 growth was 5.6 percent. Growth for 2005 is expected to reach 4.8 percent. Although the investment-to-GDP ratio has increased over the years, it stood at only 18.6 percent in 2002 and 19.5 percent in 2003, which was still relatively low for a sustained process of catch-up. However, in the second quarter of 2005, this ratio reached 23.6 percent.

Table 1. Main economic trends in Bulgaria

	units	2000	2001	2002	2003	2004
Real GDP growth rate	%	5.4	4.1	4.9	4.3	5.7*
Inflation Rate						
annual average	%	10.3	7.4	5.8	2.3	6.2
end of period	%	11.3	4.8	3.8	5.6	4.0
Unemployment reat (LFS defintion)	% of labor force	16.3	19.7	17.8	13.7	12.0
General government (ESA 95)						
budget balance	% of GDP	-0.5	1.2	-0.1	0.6	1.4
debt	% of GDP	73.6	66.2	54.0	46.3	38.8
Current account balance	% of GDP	-5.6	-7.3	-5.6	-9.3	-7.4
Gross foreign debt of the whole economy	% of GDP	86.9	78.6	65.1	60.7	63.8
Net FDI inflows (BoP data)	% of GDP	8.0	5.9	5.8	10.4	7.6

Source: Bulgarian National Bank, Ministry of Finance, National Statistical Institute
* estimate

Inflation, measured by the harmonized index of consumer prices on annual average, came down to 7.4 percent in 2001, 5.8 percent in 2002, and 2.3 percent in 2003. In 2004 inflation reached 6.2 percent. Compared to the corresponding month of the previous year, inflation was low at the end of 2001, increased to somewhat higher levels in the first quarter of 2002, following increases in indirect taxes and food pric-

Figure 1. GDP per capita 1995 - 2001 in candidate countries

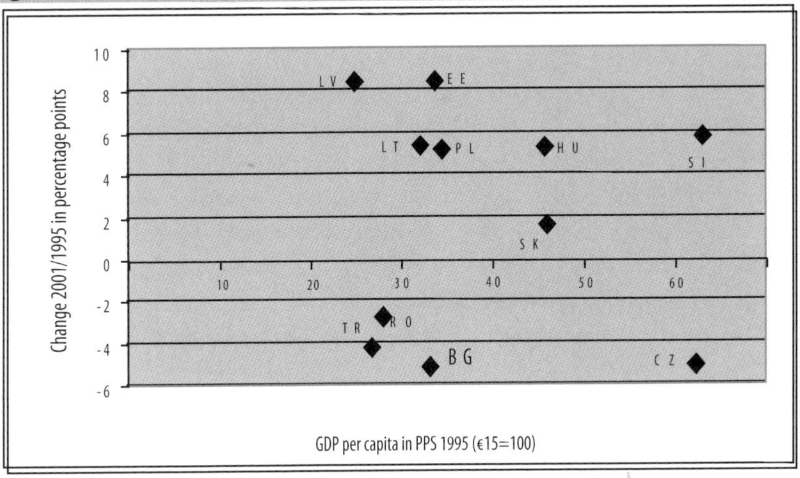

GDP per capita in PPS 1995 (€15=100)

BG-Bulgaria; EE-Estonia; HU-Hungary; LV-Latvia; LT-Lithuania; PO-Poland; RO-Romania; SK-Slovakia; SI-Slovenia; TR-Turkey

Source: Eurostat

Note: in PPS 1995 (EU15=100) and its change in percentage points

Methodological improvements in national accounts according to ESA95 and in calculating purchasing power standards are continuing. Therefore, GDP per capita in PPS is not yet fully comparable across candidate countries and over time. For the same reason, these figures will be subject to changes in the future. The year 1995 is taken as a starting point, although data are available for most countries from 1993 on, when the transition recession had bottomed out in most candidate countries. For methodological reasons, Cyprus and Malta have not been considered.

es, and declined again in the second and third quarter of 2002, also owing to lower food prices. The overall year-on-year growth of administered prices declined from three-digit rates at the beginning of 1998 to 23.3 percent in May 2002; administered prices increased by 1.7 percent in 2003 and 2.9 percent in 2004. Inflation excluding administered prices was fairly volatile, with negative rates in 1999, positive rates around 10 percent in 2000 and 2001, and a rate of 2.7 percent in May 2002. Because of higher inflation than anticipated, real short-term interest rates turned negative at the end of 2001, but became positive again in the second quarter of 2002.[4] By the end of 2004, real interest rates on some short-term lev loans were negative. The broad monetary aggregate M3 grew by 16.2 percent in nominal terms and by 13 percent in real terms between October 2001 and October 2002, and it grew by 23.1 percent in nominal terms at the end of 2004. As, under the currency board, money supply is determined exclusively by economic actors' demand for money, this shows that the economy is being re-monetized and that money demand is being re-established after its strong decline in the 1996-97 period of high inflation. The currency board arrangement continues to be well covered by foreign exchange reserves.

---

4   In terms of one-month credit and deposit rates, corrected for by consumer price index (CPI) inflation.

The high current account deficit reflects the gap between domestic savings and investment. It has been exceeded by net inflows of foreign direct investment in most of the recent years. Total foreign debt declined to below 70 percent of GDP during 2002, because of swap operations of Brady bonds against fixed-interest-rate bonds denominated in both euros and U.S. dollars in March and October 2002. In 2004, total foreign debt was 63.8 percent of GDP. Exports of goods remain low and this contributes to a high trade deficit, which is only partly balanced by exports of services, in particular tourism. In February 2003, the International Monetary Fund successfully concluded the second review of the two-year standby credit, which had been agreed one year earlier. Prior to the program's approval a Memorandum on Economic Policies of the Government and the Bulgarian National Bank had been submitted, which was reconfirmed in the context of the first review. It specifies the economic policy program based on the currency board arrangement, a cautious and flexible fiscal policy aimed at a balanced budget over the medium term and an acceleration of structural reforms to create a fully functioning and competitive market economy. In August 2004, the IMF approved a new two-year standby agreement for SDR 100 million ($146 million) to support the government's economic program for 2004-06.

In spite of some real exchange rate appreciation brought about by inflation rates exceeding those of main trade partners, international competitiveness has not deteriorated. Because of the inflation differential between the euro zone and Bulgaria, measured in terms of consumer price inflation, the Bulgarian lev experienced a real appreciation of more than 7 percent against the euro in 2000 and of almost 5 percent in 2001. The appreciation of the real effective exchange rate from mid-1997 until August 2005 was 39 percent.[5] However, since labor productivity increased more than real wages, unit labor costs at the end of 2002 were still below their level at the beginning of 1998.[6] Year-on-year growth of the real exchange rate in the third quarter of 2004 was 8.8 percent.

Unemployment increased until 2001 because of the high pace of restructuring of the economy and some regional and skills mismatch. The unemployment rate increased steadily from 12.2 percent in 1998 to 19.7 percent in 2001 in spite of high economic growth. Unemployment in 2002 was almost two percentage points lower than in 2001. In 2004, the unemployment rate was 12 percent, and by the second quarter of 2005, the unemployment rate stood at 10 percent. The employment rate of the working-age population fell from 54.5 percent in 1997 to 50.7 percent in 2001 and to 45.1 percent in the second quarter of 2005. More than 60 percent of the unemployed are long-term unemployed, and almost 23 percent of persons under twenty-five years of age are unemployed. Regional differences in unemployment are pronounced: while

---

5   Calculations by the Bulgarian National Bank (BNB).
6   Calculations by IMF.

in the southwest region the unemployment rate was 9.7 percent, in all other regions it was above 20 percent, reaching 32.8 percent in the northwest (data for level-2 statistical regions in 2001).

The level of employment in the large informal economy as well as in agriculture is difficult to assess. The presence of a large informal economy tends to add some flexibility to a labor market, which is formally rather highly regulated and characterized by high non-wage labor costs. Improved functioning of the administrative system, which will reduce the informal sector and tax evasion, should therefore go in parallel with increased labor market flexibility and lower non-wage labor costs in the formal sector of the economy. Social partners do not yet have sufficient responsibility at a decentralized level for labor relations, including wage bargaining. The proper functioning of the labor market is also hampered by the fairly low regional mobility of the workforce, caused by a combination of mentality, imperfections in the housing market, and underlying skills mismatches between regional labor demand and supply.

Fiscal policy has been prudent, as the general government deficit was below 1 percent of GDP in all years and there was even a surplus in several years. Low deficits and high nominal GDP growth contributed to a constant reduction of general government debt to a level of below 60 percent of GDP in 2002. This ratio fell further in 2004, to just under 39 percent. In 2001, the government implemented income tax reform in order both to gradually shift from direct to indirect taxation and to reduce the revenue-to-GDP ratio. Corporate and personal income tax rates are now fairly low by international standards, having been reduced by several percentage points in 2001 and 2002, to maximums of 23.5 percent and 29 percent respectively; in 2005 they were reduced again, to maximums of 15 percent and 24 percent. Value-added tax (VAT) refunding was speeded up through a further reduction of its legal deadline from four months to three and was made more resistant to fraud by an obligation to open a VAT bank account. Reforms of the pension and healthcare systems have been implemented to reduce long-term fiscal risks, but the already high social security contributions require further attention in view of an aging population. In 2002, the government kept a budgetary reserve of 0.3 percent of GDP, to be spent only if there was no deterioration of macroeconomic conditions.

To sum up, the macroeconomic picture has developed rather favorably. In the absence of monetary policy instruments and changes to exchange rates, fiscal policy has been the main instrument of macroeconomic stabilization. The tight fiscal policy pursued was appropriate in order to stabilize the currency board arrangement and to avoid a pro-cyclical stimulus to demand, which, in view of the high growth rates and the still limited capacity of the Bulgarian economy, could have triggered further inflationary pressures and an increase in the already high current account deficit. The current account deficit has so far not been a problem, since it allowed higher investment than domestic savings alone would do and was covered by net inflows of foreign direct investment in several years. In order to maintain external competitiveness vis-à-vis the euro zone as the main trading partner against which the Bulgarian lev had some real exchange rate appreciation, wage increases in the budgetary sector – which tend to serve also as a benchmark for the private sector – should remain within the limits of real productivity increases in the private sector plus the euro zone inflation rate.

Structural Reforms

The speed of structural reforms in Bulgaria in the 1990s was in parallel to its macro-economic performance. Bulgaria lagged considerably behind all other transition candidate countries (except Romania) in the mid-1990s and has only speeded up reforms since 1997. Enterprise restructuring and financial sector reform was particularly low, whereas the liberalization of foreign trade was fairly advanced. In more recent years, however, the structure of the economy has changed at a relatively fast pace. The agricultural sector's share of gross-value-added decreased dramatically, from 26.6 percent in 1997, to 12.5 percent in 2002, 11 percent in 2003, and 7.8 percent in the second quarter of 2005. This decrease is due not only to economic reform, but also to adverse weather conditions over the past few years. While industry's share (including construction) in the overall economy has increased slightly (from 27.9 percent to 31 percent) in this same period, services expanded from 45.2 percent in 1997 to 59.7 percent in 2002 and 61.2 percent in the second quarter of 2005. This sectoral shift, however, was much less pronounced in terms of employment, with more than a quarter of the labor force remaining in agriculture, and only some 3 percent shifting from industry into services.

Trade integration of the Bulgarian economy has increased. The general openness of the economy, measured by trade in goods and services as a percentage of GDP, decreased from 58 percent (1997) to 41 percent (2004) for exports and increased from 54 percent (1997) to 55 percent (2004) for imports. Bulgaria's most important export product is tourism, whose revenues accounted for about 11 percent of GDP in 2004. In the course of the abolition of tariffs in the context of the Europe Agreements, the EU has become Bulgaria's most important trading partner and the value of merchandise trade with the EU now accounts for more than half of total exports and almost half of total imports. Exported goods include mainly ores, petroleum products, pharmaceuticals, perfumes, fertilizers, textiles and clothing, footwear, iron and steel, non-ferrous metals, and machinery. Of the EU member states, Italy, Germany, and Greece have become the most important destinations for Bulgarian exports, while the most important destinations outside the EU are Russia and Turkey. With the exception of Greece, these countries had rather low economic growth in 2001, which partly explains Bulgaria's relatively weak export performance in these years. Reforms were started in 2002 to improve the functioning of customs offices, which lack the administrative capacity required for an open trade policy because of complicated and inconsistent procedures that contributed to substantial losses in the collection of VAT and excise duties.

The liberalization of prices – if measured by the number of goods and services with administered prices – has progressed, but is still incomplete. In 2001 prices for coal were liberalized, but prices for tobacco, water supply, electricity, gas, heating, medicines, postal services, and telecommunications are still administered or regulated. Measured by their shares in the consumer price index in 1997, the weight of these administered prices dropped from 14.5 percent in 1997 to 13.2 percent in 2002. However, because of their increased weight in the consumer price index, in particular because of increased demand for telecommunication services, more than one-fifth of inflation is still arising from the adjustment of administered prices. In July 2002, a three-year schedule for an increase of approximately 50 percent in electricity prices for households was decided.

Private ownership has become predominant in the economy. In 2004, 65 percent of all employees were working in the private sector. The private sector's share of gross value added grew from 63.4 percent in 1997 to 71.7 percent in 2001 and 78.5 percent in the second quarter of 2005. Houses and land are largely in private hands since land restitution was finalized in 2000. More than 90 percent of all forestland property had been returned by April 2002. Between the start of transformation and April 2002, 4821 privatization deals were concluded, representing 79.8 percent of all assets slated for privatization (that is, all assets of enterprises not on a shortlist for definitive public ownership). By December 2004, 57 percent of state enterprise assets had been sold, which represents over 85 percent of the assets that are expected to undergo privatization.

New privatization procedures were set up in the first half of 2002. These were intended to accelerate the privatization of the state-owned assets that remained (chiefly telecommunications, banking, insurance, energy, maritime transport, and tobacco) in a more transparent and efficient way through auctions, tenders, and public offerings of shares. Management or employee buyouts, which have created many problems in the past, no longer receive preferential treatment. Fifteen hundred minority stakes in companies will go to a specific segment of the stock exchange. A total of 360 companies are for direct sale and 100 are provisionally exempted from privatization either because reasons of national security make them ineligible for sale or because they first need to be restructured. However, several major privatization deals faced problems, among them the privatization of the tobacco company, which failed in early 2003.

Market entry and exit are still not working efficiently, although the situation is gradually improving. The proportion of new companies (including self-employed individuals) in the business register relative to all existing companies was 11.7 percent in 2000 and 6.6 percent in 2001. At the same time, the number of companies eliminated from the business register was 0.8 percent in 2000 and 0.7 percent in 2001. While these figures indicate high, though falling, net creation of new firms, they may also reflect both the overall business cycle and a lack of rigor in market exit procedures. Market entry is still hampered by numerous licensing procedures, which slow startups and bind considerable amounts of enterprises' and public administrations' resources. In 2002, a working group at the Ministry of Economy proposed to eliminate 74 of the 360 regimes existing at the central level and to simplify 120 of them, for which the government is carrying out the corresponding legislative procedures. Still, administrative obstacles will continue to exist at the local level. Reforms of the customs and tax administrations are ongoing in order to enhance the sometimes very poor performance of these institutions. In spite of these improvements, many businesspeople still complain about considerable problems of starting and running a business because of red tape, corruption, and slow administrative and courts procedures.

Regarding market exit, insolvency procedures continue to be slow. For the year 2002, courts statistics show that 432 insolvency cases were pending from previous years, 1707 new cases were initiated, and 1740 cases were completed, so that 399 cases were still pending at the end of the year. In order to speed up insolvency proceedings, the government amended the Commercial Code so that a company that fails to make an outstanding payment within sixty days after the date the payment was due is now considered insolvent. This change took effect in July 2003. In addition, special legal chambers have been created to deal exclusively with bankruptcy cases. A new bank bankruptcy law was adopted in September 2002, which should increase transparency and speed up procedures mainly by giving a strong control on the receivers' activities to the Banking Deposits Guarantee Fund. Although progress has been made, a number of firms are still operating at a loss, implicitly subsidized through a toleration of arrears on wages, taxes, social security contributions, and bills from state-owned suppliers, without being forced to restructure or close down.

Enforcement of property rights remains difficult in some areas. The slow proceedings of the judicial system often discourage parties from taking cases to court, which contributes to the lack of reliable enforcement. Progress has been made in reducing red tape, but these obstacles still impose substantial costs on the private sector. While large foreign companies are sometimes able to surmount these shortcomings in the legal and regulatory environment by turning directly to political decision makers, this path is not always available to smaller or domestic companies. The enforcement of intellectual property rights legislation is insufficient, and this contributes to widespread piracy and counterfeiting of software and audio-visual products. Housing property is mostly clearly defined and markets are working properly. However, in spite of the finalization of land restitution, the number of transactions and the prices of agricultural land are low as a result of a range of factors, such as fragmented land plots with often shared ownership, insufficient documentation of ownership in land registries, slow settlement of legal disputes, and low expectations of making profits in agriculture. This is a serious impediment to increasing productivity in agriculture and it is estimated that currently about 25 percent of Bulgaria's farmland is idle. Efforts are being made to modernize the land registration system, also with the support of international donors, but this takes time.

Following the crisis in 1996 and 1997, the banking sector has been restructured and is gradually developing. Since the crisis, when seventeen banks were closed down, the number of banks has stayed more or less constant (thirty-five in 2004). Following major privatizations in 2000 (Bulbank) and in 2002 (Biochim), 85 percent of commercial banking in terms of total assets was in private hands, of which about 80 percent is majority foreign-owned. The State Savings Bank (DSK), which accounted for 12 percent of total commercial banks' assets, was privatized in October 2003. The Municipal Bank of Sofia and the Encouragement Bank, whose mandate is to support SMEs, accounted for the remaining 2.5 percent of banking in state control. Banks have maintained a policy of prudent lending, which has contributed to a low rate of banking intermediation. Domestic credit as a percentage of GDP increased from 10.5 percent in 1999 to about 19 percent in 2002 and to 26 percent in 2004. The capital adequacy ratio at the end of 2004 stood at 16.58 percent. This loan restraint also keeps systemic risks to banking within close limits. The situation as regards non-performing loans steadily improved from 21.3 percent in December 1997 to 5.5 percent in December 2002 and to 2 percent by the end of 2004.[7] Interest rate spreads in terms of average short-term bank lending and deposit rates have decreased slightly, but remain high at some 10 percentage points, possibly because of the lack of alternatives to banks, but also because of the average risk profile of borrowers in the country.

The non-banking financial sector is still in its early development stage. The stock exchange remains underdeveloped and is largely illiquid with very low turnover despite a high number of companies quoted. The market capitalization of companies listed on the Bulgarian Stock Exchange was €678 million or 4.1 percent of GDP at the end of 2002. The former government intended to improve the situation by means of privatization and by gradually shifting from foreign to domestic sources of financing public debt. In fact, the stock exchange received a big boost with the privatization of the Bulgarian Telecommunications Company (BTC), and the market capitalization-to-GDP ratio reached 17.4 percent of estimated 2004 GDP. The ratio of gross

---

7   Non-performing loans are calculated as all loans not categorized as standard (i.e., assigned to watch, substandard, doubtful, or loss categories) as a percentage of all loans.

premium income of all insurance companies (including life and non-life insurance) to GDP was rather low in 2001, at 1.6 percent in 2001. In 2003, insurance companies raised $411.6 million in premiums, or 2 percent of GDP. In 2004, insurance companies raised LV834.2 million in premium revenue, or 2.2 percent of GDP.

Insufficiencies in the management of resources and demographic decline – also resulting from an emigration of young and well-educated people – underline the need for further improvements in the efficiency of spending on education.[8] Overall, Bulgaria has a well-educated and trained workforce. In 2001, according to the Labor Force Survey, 16 percent of the working-age population had tertiary education, 46 percent had secondary education, and 38 percent had primary or lower levels of education. Of those having upper secondary education, only 34 percent had a secondary vocational education. At the age of eighteen, less than half of the students remain in education, and at the age of nineteen less than a third. For low-skilled workers (those with less than upper secondary education) the unemployment rate in 2001 was a particularly high 34 percent. While Bulgarians usually score high in international surveys on mathematics and natural sciences, this is less so for social sciences. The shortage of corporate management skills and a properly trained judiciary and public administration adversely affect the performance of the economy and its competitiveness prospects. Expenditure on active labor market policies is currently about €50 million (0.34 percent of GDP), of which somewhat less than half is for recruitment subsidies for disadvantaged groups, a quarter each for support to those who are self-employed or engaged in temporary job schemes, and 5 percent for training measures.[9] The government has also introduced tax incentives for employers who finance training for their employees. Total expenditure on research and development was 0.6 percent of GDP in 1999, of which about 20 percent was spent by the business sector.

The renewal of private and public capital stock is progressing, although from a low starting level. High investment growth, supported by relatively low interest rates, has increased the ratio of gross fixed capital formation to GDP from 10.6 percent in 1997 to 19.5 percent in 2003 to 23.6 percent in the second quarter of 2005. This ratio is still on the low side in view of the continued need for high growth and catch-up. Net inflows of FDI had an important role in private capital formation since it accounted for nearly 6 percent of GDP from 1999 to 2004, peaking at almost 12 percent in 2004, and FDI related to greenfield investment was higher than privatization-related FDI in all years during that period. Accumulated FDI inflows from 1997 to 2001 were rather high at €430 per capita. However, FDI inflows in 2002 – at 3.1 percent of GDP – were somewhat lower than expected, in part because of the global economic situation and

8   Cf. World Bank (2002).

9   See also Republic of Bulgaria and European Commission (2002) for an assessment of Bulgaria's employment priorities.

the delays in privatization. FDI inflows have since picked up. For 2003, inflows reached $1.4 billion, a significant improvement over the 2002 figure of $905 million. In 2004, FDI reached nearly $2.4 billion, and for the first six months of 2005, it reached $929 million. Eighty-six percent of 2004 inflows were directed to the services sector..

The quality of infrastructure is low, but slowly improving. The overall quality of transport infrastructure is such that domestic and foreign investors see it as a major problem. Nevertheless, the infrastructure is slowly improving through the efforts of the Bulgarian authorities and support from EU pre-accession funds. The ratio of general government gross fixed capital formation to GDP varied between 3 percent and 4 percent from 1998 to 2002, up from only 1.5 percent in 1997. The length of motorways has increased from 314 to 328 kilometers, while the railway network maintained its size. The information and telecommunication structure is improving. The fixed telephone network is making some progress, but its digitalization is still low. The mobile telephone network has improved rapidly, and the sector saw the entry of a third operator, Vivatel, in October 2005. Earlier, in. In December 2004, the Commission for the Protection of Competition determined that the award of a third Global System for Mobile Communications (GSM) license to the buyer of the Bulgarian Telecommunications Company, Viva Ventures (which owns 65 percent of Vivatel), did not constitute illegitimate state aid, thereby clearing the way for the company to build its own GSM network. Internet use continues to grow, albeit from a very low level. Energy infrastructure investment is oriented toward improving quality and connecting networks to neighboring countries. Local infrastructure, such as streets, sewerage, water supply, and schools, is often in a poor state since municipalities have few funds for investment.

Enterprise restructuring has made progress, mostly in the context of privatization, but restructuring is still unfinished in some sectors. Energy efficiency is still very low. In the electricity sector, the government has adopted a new strategy based on the institutional separation of generation, transmission, and distribution. Transmission infrastructure will remain regulated and state owned, while generation and distribution are being liberalized in order to allow third-party access, initially only for costumers whose annual consumption exceeds certain thresholds. Privatization of the seven regional electricity distribution companies occurred in 2004, and restructuring is ongoing in the gas sector, coal mines, and district heating companies. There has been further progress in restructuring the steel industry, though several privatized enterprises still depend on soft budget constraints in the form of wage, tax, and customs duty arrears. In the transport sector, several state-owned enterprises still continuously make losses. On 1 January 2002, the institutional separation of the railway infrastructure and operations was legally completed, which formally ended the state monopoly on rail transport.

Small and medium-sized enterprises have not yet developed their full potential for growth and employment. The share of enterprises with fewer than 250 employees accounted for 35 percent of the gross value added and for 56 percent of employment in 1997, and increased to 43 percent of the gross value added and 65 percent of employment in 2000. In spite of this positive development, it is still insufficient to compensate for the substantial job losses of large enterprises following their privatization and restructuring. One explanation is that SMEs tend to suffer from the worst aspects of the often difficult conditions of doing business in Bulgaria, including red tape, corruption, and lack of access to financing, information, and management skills. Banks often refuse to grant loans to SMEs because they have overly high requirements for collateral, which is difficult to use given the shortcomings of the judicial system, and because many firms' accounts do not look promising, since they understate their figures in order to avoid taxes. The government has created a micro-lending scheme and a guarantee fund, but the number of beneficiaries and the effects on economic development remain limited.

The state is gradually reducing its involvement in the productive sector. Privatization and trade liberalization have been the most important reductions of state intervention. Hidden subsidies in the form of tax and social securities arrears as well as debt to state-owned suppliers have decreased, but still amounted to 1.6 percent of GDP for tax arrears and 0.7 percent of GDP for social security arrears. The energy and transport sectors still receive substantial amounts of state aid to cover losses. A new law on

Table 2: PEP 2004 – Fiscal projections

	2003	2004	2005	2006	2007	Δ 2003-2007
Revenues	40.9	40.4	38.2	38.2	40.0	-0.9
of which:						
Taxes and social security contributions	32.3	32.3	30.8	31.1	31.2	-1.1
Other (residual)	8..6	8.1	7.4	7.1	8.8	0.2
Expenditure	41.0	40.3	38.6	38.2	41.3	0.3
of which:						
Primary expenditure	38.9	38.1	36.5	35.9	39.1	0.2
of which:						
Gross fixed capital formation	2.8	3.5	3.7	3.7	4.6	1.8
Consumption	10.3	9.9	9.6	9.4	9.5	-0.8
Transfers & subsidies	18.3	17.3	16.2	16.1	16.5	-1.8
Other (residual)	7.5	7.4	7.0	6.7	8.5	1.0
Interest payments	2.1	2.1	2.1	2.3	2.3	0.2
Budget Balance	-0.1	0.1	-0.5	0.0	-1.3	-1.2
Cyclically adjusted	0.7	0.2	-0.1	0.2	-1.3	-2.0
Primary balance	2.0	2.1	1.7	2.3	0.9	-1.1
Gross debt level	48.4	40.8	37.4	34.2	32.5	-15.9

Sources: Pre-accession Economic Programme (PEP), ECFIN calculations

state aid, which entered into force in June 2002, provides a good procedural framework for state aid control, but still requires the adoption of clear implementing provisions. The Ministry of Finance has maintained the financial discipline of state-owned enterprises by monitoring closely their use of credits and wage increases. Nevertheless, the state remains responsive to sector-specific requests for protection, for example by introducing up to 40 percent protective import duties for nitrogen fertilizers as of July 2002. The government also intends to retain golden shares after the privatization of the tobacco and telecom monopolies. The agricultural sector, including tobacco production, also increasingly benefits from subsidies.

Conclusion and Outlook

Compared to the general reform agenda of economic transition as sketched earlier, under "Basic Aspects of Economic Reforms," Bulgaria has already progressed considerably, but many things still remain to be done. Among the main achievements reviewed above are macroeconomic stabilization, reduced size of the government sector, real estate restitution, privatization, substantial domestic and foreign investment, financial sector restructuring, and a high degree of external liberalization. However, further progress is necessary in particular on the enforceability of property rights, market entry and exit procedures, the flexibility of the labor market, the deepening of the capital market, the functioning of the land market, and the quality of infrastructure and human capital. These reforms will increase the flexibility of an economy tied up in a currency board arrangement where the nominal exchange rate is not available to adjust to external shocks.

Table 3: PEP 2004 – Economic projections

	2003	2004	2005	2006	2007
Real GDP (% change)	4.3	5.0	5.3	5.3	5.5
Contributions					
Final domestic demand	8.2	7.5	6.7	6.8	7.1
Change in inventories	0.7	0.2	-0.6	-0.2	-0.2
External balance of goods and services	-4.6	-2.7	-0.8	-1.4	-1.4
Employment (% change)	2.9	1.5	2.0	1.5	1.5
Unemployment (%)	13.7	12.4	11.6	10.7	10.0
GDP deflator (% change)	2.1	5.1	3.5	3.7	4.0
CPI inflation (%)	2.4	6.3	3.7	3.6	4.0
Current account balance (% of GDP	-8.5	-8.8	-8.3	-8.0	-7.0
Source:Pre-accession Economic Programme (PEP) 2004					

As a medium-term outlook, the Bulgarian authorities submitted their latest pre-accession economic program (PEP) to the European Commission at the end of 2004, which confirmed the former government's commitment to its reform agenda. The high fiscal discipline envisaged by the scenario for the medium-term fiscal policy, targeting a balanced budget by 2006, will contribute to a balanced macroeconomic policy mix and a further reduction of the tax burden (see table 2). The PEP also presents the agenda for further structural reforms and includes an estimation of their fiscal implications. The projections in the PEP for the various indicators are given in table 3, showing that – even with rather high real GDP growth rates – a sound process of economic catch-up takes many years.

The continuation of the reform process toward maintaining macroeconomic stability and improving the efficiency of markets will have at least three positive effects on the Bulgarian economy. First, it further enhances investors' confidence in the Bulgarian economy and provides good conditions for a further buildup of the capital stock, which is indispensable for the sustained process of catching up. Second, it underpins the sustainability of the currency board arrangement and makes any discussions on a change in the exchange rate regime obsolete. Third, it makes the objective of Bulgaria's accession to the EU in 2007 – as supported by the European Council in December 2002 – a realistic perspective.

References

Economist Intelligence Unit. 2005. Country Report: Bulgaria (October).

European Commission. 2002. *2002 regular report on Bulgaria's progress towards accession* {COM(2002) 700 final}(October). Brussels.

Nsouli, Saleh M., Mounir Rached, and Norbert Funke. 2002. The speed of adjustment and the sequencing of economic reforms: issues and guidelines for policymakers. IMF Working Paper WP/02/132. Washington, D.C.

Republic of Bulgaria, 2004 *Pre-accession economic programme (2004-2007).* Sofia.

Republic of Bulgaria and European Commission. 2002. Joint assessment of employment priorities in Bulgaria.

http://europa.eu.int/comm/employment_social/employment_analysis/japs/bulgaria_en.pdf..

World Bank. 2002. *Bulgaria – Public expenditure issues and directions for reform – A public expenditure and institutional review.* Report 23979-BUL. Washington, D.C.

7 Bulgaria: Transition Success and Challenges Ahead

By Elisabetta Falcetti, Principal Economist,
European Bank for Reconstruction and Development

Edited and updated paper based on the conference[1]

During the first decade of transition, the Bulgarian economy successfully withstood the economic recession that followed the 1996 financial crisis and the Kosovo crisis of 1999, and is now heading down a path of real growth convergence with the countries of the European Union (EU). Significant progress in structural reforms has recently been made in many areas, including the liberalization of markets and trade, the privatization of small and medium enterprises (SMEs), and the restructuring of the financial sector. However, a previously irresolute transition process has left Bulgaria economically behind other countries in Central and Eastern Europe and the Baltics (CEB). Corporate governance and enterprise restructuring are weak, and financial intermediation is still low compared to the other EU accession countries of CEB, as banks remain very cautious in their lending activities. This chapter presents a brief overview of the major successes achieved during the first decade of transition, and the key transition challenges ahead for Bulgaria. The main topics covered are macroeconomic developments since 1996; key reform progress as measured by the EBRD transition indicators; the main transition challenges ahead, with emphasis on the need for improving the domestic business climate in Bulgaria; and the EBRD's role in the country, as defined in the 2003 Country Strategy (EBRD 2003a).

A Successful Macroeconomic Stabilization

Over the last few years, Bulgaria has made an important and successful turnaround, thanks to the strong financial discipline imposed by the adoption of the currency board regime in 1997 and the implementation of sound economic policies and structural reforms afterwards.

By the end of 1998, the economy had fully recovered from the recession and hyperinflation that characterized the aftermath of the 1996 crisis, owing to the implementation of strict monetary and fiscal policies. GDP has grown on average at 4.4 percent

---

1   The views expressed in this paper are those of the author only and not of the EBRD.

per year since 1998 and is expected to remain strong as convergence with the EU starts to come into play. So far, the economy has proven to be quite resilient to the world-wide decline in growth, especially in the EU, which is Bulgaria's main trading partner. This is largely due to the fact that GDP growth has been driven by the strong rebound in domestic demand and, in particular, higher investment in gross fixed capital formation, while the fiscal tightening reduced the share of household consumption in GDP growth. This, in turn, should lead to an increase in both industrial production and future export capacity. On the supply side, GDP growth was driven by increased activity in the industrial and services sectors. In 2003, real GDP growth was 4.3 percent and 5.6 percent in 2004. The Economist Intelligence Unit expects this measure to grow by 5.7 percent in 2005.

Inflation was sharply brought down from 579 percent at the end of 1997 to 0.9 percent at the end of 1998, thanks to the introduction of the currency board regime in July 1997. Since then, inflation has been in the single digits except for a peak in 2000 of 11.4 percent. A combination of higher than expected oil prices and a severe drought that hit the Balkan region contributed to the upsurge in inflation in 2000. The negative trend was reversed in 2001, after which the inflation rate gradually declined to reach 3.9 percent at the end of 2002, despite increases in the price of electricity, central heating, and a number of administered goods, including medicines and tobacco. The increase recorded at the end of 2003 was mainly due to higher energy and food prices in the last quarter of the year. These factors contributed to an end-year infla-

Table 1. Bulgaria selected economic indicators, 1996-2003

	1996	1997	1998	1999	2000	2001	2002	2003
Real GDP, percent change	-9.4	-5.6	4.0	2.3	5.4	4.0	4.8	4.3
Inflation, (percent, end-year)	310.8	578.6	0.9	6.2	11.4	4.8	3.9	5.6
Budget balance (percent of GDP)	-10.3	-2.4	1.0	-0.9	-1.0	-0.9	-0.6	0.0
Domestic credit (end year, percent of GDP)	115.2	22.5	16.0	16.0	18.7	20.9	25.2	29.8
Domestic credit to the private sector (end-year, percent of GDP)	35.3	5.6	8.0	10.4	11.9	14.3	18.7	27.6
Trade balance (percent of GDP)	1.9	3.7	-3.0	-8.3	-9.3	-11.5	-10.4	-12.5
Current account balance (percent of GDP)	0.2	4.1	-0.5	-5.3	-5.6	-6.5	-4.4	-8.4
Net foreign direct investment ($ million)	138	507	537	789	1003	641	570	1419
Gross external debt (public and private, percent of GDP)	97	93.7	80.6	78.7	88.9	78.3	70.3	66.4
Gross reserves (end-year, in months of imports of goods and services)	1.0	4.4	5.4	5.3	5.4	5.0	5.8	6.0

Source: European Bank of Reconstruction and Development (EBRD)

tion rate of 5.6 percent in 2003. Inflation in December 2004 fell to 4 percent. Since the 1996 crisis, confidence in the banking system has improved and strong domestic credit growth is sustaining domestic demand. Despite the fast increase in credit to the private sector recorded in 2001 and early 2002, its ratio over GDP was still below 25 percent in December 2002 and was low compared to other accession countries in Central and Eastern Europe. The trend is increasing, however, since in 2003 the ratio reached nearly 30 percent and 37.1 percent in 2004.

Under the International Monetary Fund (IMF) program, authorities made a commitment to maintain a prudent fiscal policy and have successfully contained the consolidated budget deficit below 1 percent of GDP since 1998, reaching a full balance in 2003. The government's tax policy aims at gradually decreasing direct taxation (of both personal income and corporate profits) and at increasing indirect taxes (value-added taxes and excises). Debt ratios have been historically high in Bulgaria. However, the combination of a more active debt management policy and the recent appreciation of the euro has reduced the ratio of total government debt (including domestic and external debt) over GDP to about 41 percent of 2004 GDP, from more than 300 percent in 1996. Total gross external debt (public and private) over GDP also improved dramatically, decreasing to 70 percent of GDP in 2004 from 97 percent of GDP in 1996. The debt repayment capacity of the country is fairly good and the fiscal reserves accumulated by the government were projected at about €2 billion at the end of 2003. Authorities are highly committed to maintaining the currency board regime, and the stock of foreign international reserves of the central bank recovered to $6 billion at the end of November 2003, or six months of imports of goods and services, up from $560 million in the aftermath of the 1996 crisis. Reserves increased further in 2004, to $9.2 billion at the end of November 2004, or over eight months of imports of goods and services.

Despite the successful macroeconomic stabilization, Bulgaria's external financing position remains vulnerable to a protracted slowdown of the world economy or a sudden change in investor confidence regarding emerging markets. Higher oil prices and import demand, fuelled by the rapid growth in credit to the non-government sector, led to this deterioration in the external position in 2003. As imports grew faster than exports, the trade deficit reached $2.5 billion at the end of December 2003 and $3.4 billion in 2004. High income receipts from a good tourism season and increased remittances should help contain the current account deficit, which is nonetheless projected at 8.8 percent of GDP for 2005. The EU accounts for more than 50 percent of Bulgarian trade flows. However, the increasing share of exports to Central European Free Trade Association (CEFTA)[2] countries highlights the important role that

---

2   CEFTA is a multilateral agreement for creation of a free-trade zone by a gradual removal of duties for industrial goods, liberalization of trade for agricultural products, and free competition on the territories of the member countries. These are Bulgaria, the Czech Republic, Hungary, Poland, Romania, the Slovak Republic, and Slovenia.

regional integration can play in mitigating the impact of the world slowdown on the Bulgarian economy. The main sources of financing remain foreign direct investment (FDI) flows and official international funds (World Bank, IMF, and EU pre-accession funds). However, with privatization of large-scale enterprises (excluding public utilities) coming to an end, attracting increasing greenfield FDI is becoming a key challenge for Bulgaria.

Looking forward, the economic outlook remains positive. Annual growth is likely to remain in the range of 4 percent to 4.5 percent in the near term, as investment needs pick up ahead of EU accession, and net exports benefit from the expected moderate recovery of the EU markets. Over the longer run, advances in structural reforms are needed to bring about further productivity increases, as positive wage differentials with the EU will gradually narrow. The external position remains vulnerable to a delayed recovery in the EU, higher oil prices, or further delays in some of the key privatizations.

Reform Progress

The EBRD Transition Reports have assessed progress in reforms since 1994 in all twenty-seven transition countries where it operates. The three dimensions of a market economy that have been evaluated are the following: markets and trade, enterprises, and financial institutions[3]. The EBRD transition indicators measure how much progress has been made in each of these areas toward achieving a well-functioning market economy. Progress is measured against the standards of industrialized market economies, keeping in mind that there is neither a perfectly functioning market economy nor a unique endpoint for transition. Each transition indicator varies on a scale from 1 to 4+, where 1 represents little or no change from a planned economy and a 4+ represents the standard of an advanced market economy[4]. Scores with a plus or minus attached are translated into numerical values by adding or subtracting 0.33.

The average transition indicator for a country is defined thereafter as the simple average of the following eight sub-components: large and small-scale privatization, governance and enterprise restructuring, price and trade liberalization, competition policy, banking reform, and, finally, security markets and non-bank financial institutions[5].

---

3   A fourth dimension, infrastructure, was added more recently and the indicators back-dated to 1994. However, the analysis in this paper abstracts from this dimension.

4   These are ordinal indexes, and therefore the scores are not directly comparable across different dimensions of transition. That means that moving from a score of 1 to 2 is not necessarily the same as moving from 3 to 4, and a score of 3 in one dimension, e.g. price liberalization, is not equivalent to a 3 in banking reform.

5   Table A1 in the appendix to this chapter describes the full classification system for each of these indicators.

Figure 1. Average transition indicators for transition countries

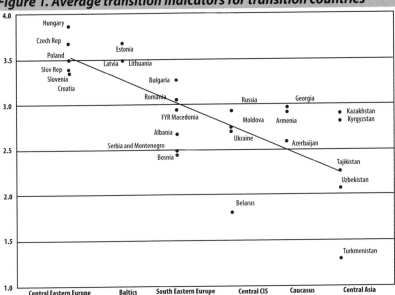

Figure 1 plots the average transition indicators for the twenty-seven transition countries in which the EBRD operates grouped by main geographical areas. These are Central and Eastern Europe, the Baltic countries, Southeastern Europe (SEE), central Commonwealth of Independent States (CIS) countries, the Caucasus, and Central Asia. The chart shows that there is a significant variation in reform progress across the six subregions. The countries of Central Eastern Europe and the Baltics (CEB) have progressed the furthest in all aspects of reform while countries in the CIS continue to lag behind. Those in SEE lie somewhat in the middle, with Bulgaria closing the gap with the group of advanced reformers in CEB, followed by Romania, the other EU accession country of SEE. These geographical differences have now persisted for several years, reflecting the much more rapid progress in reforms in CEB during the mid-1990s. However, since 2001 several of the less advanced transition economies in SEE and CIS, including Bulgaria, have started to catch up with the frontrunner EU accession countries of CEB.

The average EBRD transition indicators in figure 1 mask, however, considerable differences between the various areas of reform within countries. A distinction commonly referred to in the transition economic literature is the one between "first phase" reforms, which take priority during the early years of transition, and "second phase" reforms. First-phase reforms include price liberalization, trade and exchange rate liberalization, and small-scale privatization. These reforms have been largely completed in most countries in the region, with the exception of some of the CIS countries where market liberalization has not been fully achieved yet. Second-phase reforms, which began at different times across the region, focus instead on institution building. They involve competition policy, enterprise restructuring, large-scale privatization,[6] and the development of banking and non-bank financial institutions. These reforms have shown to be considerably more difficult to implement because they require significant administrative capacity and they may face high resistance from vested interest groups who would benefit from maintaining the status quo.

Table 2 presents the transition indicators scores of Bulgaria and contrasts them to those of the other EU accession countries of the region. These indexes can be used to assess relative performance across countries along various reforms' dimensions, and can be used to assess progress in initial and second phase reforms.

As shown in table 2, first-phase reforms (price and trade liberalization together with small-scale privatization), had almost been completed in Bulgaria by mid-2002. Since the 1996 crisis, the country has made impressive progress in social and structural reforms, which allowed Bulgaria to catch up substantially with the more advanced transition countries of CEB. As a result, the banking system was completely restructured and rehabilitated and most of the loss-making state-owned companies have been closed down. Small-scale privatization is nearing completion and the present government is committed to moving ahead swiftly with the privatization of the reflected in the high scores attained by Bulgaria in the areas that fall under the definition of first-phase reforms (see first three columns of table 2).

Though not invited to join the EU at its Copenhagen summit in December 2002, Bulgaria is a firm candidate for membership in 2007.[7] The completion of the accession process to the EU would not only require substantial additional investments in infrastructure and environment, but also institution building and in particular the reform of Bulgaria's administration and judicial systems. With corruption being a source of major public concern, regulatory reforms are needed to improve law enforcement and overall governance. In order to boost private investment and attract more FDI, Bulgaria needs to push ahead firmly the second-phase reform agenda and build the foundations of a well-functioning market economy. As shown in table 2, Bulgaria still scores below the average of the more advanced EU accession candidates of CEB in the areas of governance and enterprise restructuring, competition policy, and financial sector development. The achieved political stability and the goal of EU accession will play a key role in driving Bulgaria's transition process in the years ahead.

---

6   While we acknowledge that in some countries large-scale mass privatizations occurred in an early stage of transition, in the majority of transition countries large-scale privatization has been slow and deferred to the second phase of transition. This explains why large-scale privatization is included here among the second-phase reforms.

7   In June 2004 Bulgaria and the EU concluded the country's accession negotiations with the closing of the final two chapters of the acquis communautaire, ensuring its accession in 2007.

Table 2: EBRD transition indicators of EU accession countries, 200

	Small-scale priv.	Price liber.	Trade & foreign esch. sys.	Large-scale priv	Governance & enterprise restruct.	Competition policy	Banking reform & interest rate liber.	Securities markets & non-bank financial inst.
Bulgaria	4-	4+	4+	4-	3-	2+	3+	2+
Czech Republic	4+	4+	4+	4	3+	3	4-	3
Estonia	4+	4	4+	4	3+	3-	4-	3+
Hungary	4+	4+	4+	4	3+	3	4	4-
Latvia	4+	4+	4+	3+	3	3-	4-	3
Lithuania	4+	4+	4+	4-	3	3	3	3
Poland	4+	4+	4+	3+	3+	3	3+	4-
Romania	4-	4+	4	3+	2	2+	3-	2
Slovak Republic	4+	4+	4+	4	3	3	3+	3-
Slovenia	4+	4	4+	3	3	3-	3+	3-

Note: The index ranges from 1, indicating little or no progress, to 4+, pointing to standards similar to advanced economies. The classification system is presented in table A1 of the appendix to this chapter.

Source: EBRD (2003b).

Bulgaria is now facing a unique opportunity to build on progress achieved thus far and to move the reform agenda forward by capitalizing on good macroeconomic performance and political stability. The key transition challenges ahead are 1) to maintain macroeconomic stability in the wake of increased global uncertainty and decreased appetite for emerging-markets risk; and 2) to complete implementation of the reform agenda in view of EU accession in 2007.

Maintaining *tight fiscal discipline* in support of the currency board arrangement (CBA) is key to achieving the first objective. This in turn will entail containing future public sector wage increases, reducing the government quasi-fiscal deficit fuelled by the large budgetary deficits of Bulgarian municipalities and public utilities, and aiming for a balanced budget in the medium/long-term horizon. These measures are necessary to sustain the CBA, which as pointed out by Buiter and Grafe (2002), "is a dual commitment to an exchange rate rule and a budgetary or fiscal rule." While the exchange rate rule is a commitment to maintain a fixed exchange rate against a reference currency or basket of currencies, the fiscal rule preempts the central bank from being a creditor of last resort and imposes full backing of the monetary base by at least an equivalent stock of international reserves. This dual commitment also represents the dual challenge of containing domestic cost and price pressures (that is, maintaining international competitiveness through increases in productivity) and avoiding domestic credit creation by the central bank.

In line with the objective of fiscal consolidation is the government's public debt management strategy, which aims at reducing Bulgaria's public debt ratios to Maastricht levels, increasing the average maturity of the existing debt stock, and shifting its currency composition away from the U.S. dollar and toward the reserve currency, the euro.

Another key precondition for maintaining macroeconomic stability in Bulgaria over the medium term is to attract *increasing FDI inflows* to finance the high current account deficits without having to rely on further debt issuances. This has proven to be a difficult task for Bulgaria in the most recent past, thanks to a combination of unfavorable external conditions, with investors pulling out from emerging markets at large, and the difficult investment climate in the country. As shown in figure 2, until 2000 net FDI inflows to Bulgaria have always been in excess of the current account financing needs. However, from 2001-03, net FDI inflows fell short of the current account deficit.

The sale of a 65-percent stake in the Bulgarian Telecommunications Company (BTC) was completed in June 2004. It was unlikely that the former government would complete the privatization of the tobacco company Bulgartabac in 2004, but by the end of December 2004, 57 percent of state enterprise assets had been sold. This figure represents 85 percent of the assets that are expected to undergo privatization. Evidence indicates that the former government strongly favored strategic foreign investors for the companies remaining to be privatized. However, with the privatization process nearing completion, it is key that Bulgaria continue to attract a stable, and possibly larger, inflow of greenfield and brownfield FDI.

A necessary pre-condition for FDI inflows to take off in Bulgaria is a general *improvement in the country's investment climate,* which means tackling corruption and providing a transparent and predictable operational environment for private business. Excessive government control together with an unclear interpretation of existing laws and a weak judiciary system are among the major obstacles faced by investors in Bulgaria. Related to this point is the need to *promote institution building and public sector reform* (including a reform of the judiciary) to create the right incentives and to develop a culture of accountability in the public sector. Despite significant progress in building the legislative and regulatory framework to support private sector activity, there is still scope to improve the effectiveness of its application and implementation. Administrative procedures need to become more business friendly and business establishment and registration procedures need to be further streamlined.

These views have been confirmed by the findings of the Business Environment and Enterprise Performance Survey (BEEPS), launched by the EBRD and the World Bank in 1999 and then repeated in 2002 by surveying close to six thousand firms across twenty-six countries in the region, including Bulgaria. The BEEPS asked

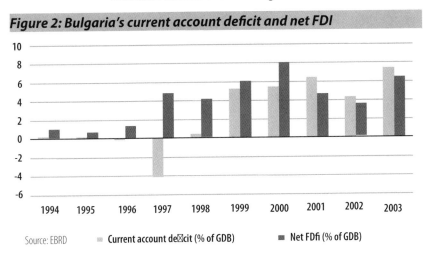

Figure 2: Bulgaria's current account deficit and net FDI

Source: EBRD — Current account deficit (% of GDB) — Net FDfi (% of GDB)

entrepreneurs to evaluate economic governance and state institutions and to assess the extent to which the business environment creates obstacles to the operation and growth of their businesses. The information on reform progress contained in these survey data is therefore complementary to that derived from the EBRD transition indicators (see "Reform Progress," above). Indeed, the last ones do not fully address important aspects of economic governance, such as taxation, business regulation, corruption, and the rule of law, and do not take account of the two-way relationship between enterprises and the state.

In particular, the 1999 and 2002 BEEPS asked firms to assess how the functioning of the state, physical infrastructure, and financial institutions affect their business operations. Seven broad areas, directly or indirectly related to the functioning of the state and public administration, were assessed. They include taxation, business regulation, the judiciary, crime, corruption, finance, and infrastructure. Firms were asked to assess how problematic these factors are for the operation and growth of their business on a scale of 1 to 4, where a score of 1 represents a minor obstacle and a score of 4 indicates a major obstacle.

Figure 3 summarizes the average responses to the business environment questions of the 250 Bulgarian firms interviewed in the 2002 round of BEEPS, and compares it to the 1999 replies. A number of caveats must be taken into account before analyzing these data. First, although the selection criteria were the same, the two rounds of BEEPS are not strictly directly comparable because 1) the sample of interviewed enterprises is different for each round and 2) the formulation of the questionnaire was modified between 1999 and 2002. Nonetheless, it has been possible to reconcile the replies within the seven broad areas of corporate governance described above and illustrated in the figure. Second, as explained in the EBRD Transition Report for 2002 (EBRD 2002), a first comparison of the 1999 and 2002 BEEPS suggested that the business cycle may strongly influence people's perceptions of the business environment. Therefore, in order to compare the underlying quality of the business environment across countries and over time, some statistical adjustments on the 1999 and 2002 BEEPS data have been made, so as to isolate the influence of the business cycle from the qualitative judgments. Adjusted results were used to construct business environment scores that reflect the business climate that would prevail if all countries shared the same macroeconomic performance[8].

The results from the BEEPS surveys shown in figure 3 confirm the progress that has been made in economic governance over the past three years in Bulgaria, complementing the EBRD's transition indicators' assessment of progress in transition. The 2002 BEEPS shows that the business environment has improved significantly across almost all dimensions since 1999, and that this improvement is not only due to the economic recovery enjoyed by the country since 1999. In particular, the fight against corruption seems to have borne some fruits, because from being perceived as the major obstacle to doing business in Bulgaria in 1999, this indicator is now ranked third. According to the 2002 results, access to finance appears to be the major obstacle to starting a new business in Bulgaria. Although improved with respect to 1999, taxation remains the second most important obstacle, with an average response of 2.36 in 2002, against 3.01 in 1999. The largest improvement was recorded in quality of and access to infrastructure, including telecommunication, electricity, and transportation.

The results from the BEEPS surveys highlight the need to improve access to finance by *increasing intermediation through banks and by promoting the development of the non-banking financial sector, along with the domestic capital market* in Bulgaria. After the banking sector almost collapsed in early 1997, substantial progress has been made in the consolidation and privatization of the financial sector. On the whole, banks are now highly capitalized, and non-performing loans continue to decline. The sale of the country's largest bank, Bulbank, in mid-2000, of Biochim in 2002, and of DSK, the former savings bank, in 2003 marked the end of the privatization process in the banking sector. The Bulgarian National Bank's regulatory and supervisory systems are considered among the better developed in

---

8   This involved running a regression of the qualitative assessments of the business environment at the firm level on the characteristics of firms (size, ownership, and location within a country), reported quantitative measures of the businesses environment that relate to the qualitative assessments, the average growth rate over the past year, and country dummy variables to allow for any other country-specific effects. The predicted values from this regression were then used to derive "adjusted" qualitative business environment assessments, which control for the business cycle by setting the macroeconomic growth rate to be equal to the average of all countries.

Figure 3: Business environment over time in Bulgaria

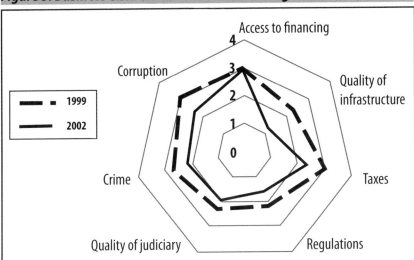

the region. However, despite these achievements, the sector still faces a number of challenges, including further consolidation, increased lending, and product diversification. Increased foreign ownership is bringing both capital and know-how to the largest banks: foreign-owned banks now control more than 85 per cent of the banking sector assets. The smaller banks, both locally owned and foreign, are expected to grow by consolidation and specialization in order to ensure their long-term competitiveness. The need for increased financial intermediation is demonstrated by the fact that the total assets of the banking sector represented only 45 percent of Bulgaria's GDP in 2002. This ratio reached 50 percent in 2003 and 66 percent in 2004. Although improving, lending levels remain on the low side. On one hand, at the enterprise level, this is caused by the lack of transparency and sophistication in preparing business plans. On the other, although banks are building management know-how and credit skills, they remain over-prudent. This is often coupled with lack of access to longer-term funding. The product range of most Bulgarian banks also remains extremely limited. New products, both deposit and credit related, need to be introduced, which is beginning to happen in the recently privatized banks in the form of consumer lending and mortgage facilities. The pace of such developments is constrained, however, by the restructuring needs of these institutions. Furthermore, the availability of alternative sources of financing, as well as of local and regional funding sources is still very limited in Bulgaria, and targeted efforts should be made to develop those financial vehicles.

Perhaps the major challenge ahead in this area is to promote the development of the non-banking financial sector, including full implementation of insurance and pension reforms. Following the overall successful introduction of both voluntary and mandatory pension reforms (pillar 2 and pillar 3), it is imperative that the sector be strengthened through consolidation. There are many funds with only a small number of participants, which calls their long-term viability into question. In order to ensure that members obtain a reasonable return, smaller funds are likely to merge amongst themselves or to be acquired by larger funds. The Bulgarian insurance market remains underdeveloped, both in terms of foreign involvement and in terms of product depth. Insurance penetration, including health insurance, remains one of the lowest in the region as a percentage of GDP, and both business and consumer markets remain heavily underinsured. While positive developments in the banking sector have induced some changes in the insurance sector (such as the introduction of new products) it will take some time for an insurance culture to become embedded into Bulgarian society.

Role of the EBRD

The EBRD is a major foreign investor in Bulgaria and is proactively committed to supporting FDI. The bank's position as a major catalyst for investment in Bulgaria (cumulative business volume of €1 billion as of December 2003, as part of total funds mobilized of more than $2 billion) underlines its important role. In line with the transition challenges highlighted in the previous section of this paper, the EBRD operational priorities, as outlined in the 2003 Bulgaria Country Strategy (EBRD 2003a), are private sector development and infrastructure:

- **Private sector development**. The main challenges associated with the development of the private sector in Bulgaria are still a relatively poor investment climate and a lack of transparency. Poor corporate governance and management skills, and a shortage of long-term financing continue to be serious constraints for attracting investment capital to the country. These factors explain why FDI levels in Bulgaria have been historically low (totaling approximately $8.4 billion in cumulative terms from 1992 to September 2004) and why several entities in the country remain in state hands. The EBRD is involved in privatization and post-privatization projects in the industrial and agribusiness sectors, primarily with foreign strategic investors. The bank will seek to play a key role in promoting post-privatization investment and greenfield private sector projects, looking to attract new FDI to industry, tourism, agribusiness, and natural resources. The EBRD will broaden its geographical coverage of the micro, small, and medium-sized private enterprises through a careful selection of additional Bulgarian partner banks benefiting from SME credit lines. Technical assistance is provided to support institution building and the implementation of effective and efficient lending programs. The bank will also emphasize supporting the development of the non-banking financial sector, including the development of a three-pillar pension system, private insurance markets, leasing, and mortgage financing.

- **Infrastructure.** In the last several years the EBRD has focused its activities on developing private and non-sovereign projects in the infrastructure sector. The bank's first priority will be to support the privatization of the energy sector, both in generation and distribution, as well as financing new generation capacity. Given Bulgaria's high energy intensity (one of the highest in the world), the EBRD will promote improvements in energy efficiency and renewable energy resources. Capitalizing on its experience to date, the bank will support rehabilitation and commercialization of the district heating networks. Close cooperation will be maintained with the donor community of the Kozloduy International Decommissioning Support Fund established at the EBRD in order to provide grant financing for the decommissioning of unsafe nuclear units, and energy and energy efficiency measures consequential to the closure of nuclear units. Furthermore, the bank will continue its dialogue with the authorities to promote improvements to the legal and regulatory framework in the sector. By directly providing investment financing to municipalities and municipal and regional utilities without a state guarantee, the bank will support the decentralization of financing responsibilities and will contribute to the enhancement of the creditworthiness of municipal borrowers, thereby developing their long-term capacity for financing capital improvements on a sustainable basis. The EBRD will encourage the development of an effective regulatory regime fully consistent with EU accession principles and demonstrably independent of government.

Conclusions

Over the past few years Bulgaria has achieved solid economic growth and made progress in economic reform. The goal of EU accession in 2007 has driven reform efforts toward institution building and public administration reform.

However, the country is still lagging behind the first wave of EU accession countries in areas such as corporate governance and enterprise restructuring, competition policy, and financial sector development. Access to financing is still perceived as the major obstacle to doing business in Bulgaria, while significant progress has been recorded in fighting corruption and street crime. This is evidence that has emerged from the second round of the Business Environment and Enterprise Performance Survey, run by the EBRD and the World Bank in 1999 and 2002. According to the sample of 250 Bulgarian firms interviewed, the business environment has improved significantly in Bulgaria along all dimensions, and improvements have been particularly notable in access to and quality of the infrastructure and the fight against corruption. To some extent, these improvements simply reflect the better macroeconomic environment, which may encourage firms to be more optimistic. However, there have been some actual improvements too, as the burden of taxation and corruption has declined. Moreover, a more level playing field for different types of firms is beginning to emerge.

Developments in the frontrunner EU accession countries suggest that the task of institution building will remain at the core of the policy agenda for Bulgaria for some time to come. Even with the strong influence provided by the *acquis communautaire*, institutional weaknesses remain in regulation, competition policy, the judicial system, and often in local government administration. The improvements of the past few years call for continued progress and awareness that the task of transition has not been completed.

Classification System for Transition Indicators

Transition Element	Category	Description of category
Large-scale privatization	1	Little private ownership
	2	Comprehensive scheme almost ready for implementation; some sales completed
	3	More than 25 per cent of large-scale enterprise assets in private hands or in the process of being privatized (with the process having reached a stage at which the state has effectively ceded its ownership rights), but possibly with major unresolved issues regarding corporate governance
	4	More than 50 per cent of state-owned enterprise and farm assets in private ownership and significant progress on corporate governance of these enterprises
	4+	Standards and performance typical of advanced industrial economies: more than 75 per cent of enterprise assets in private ownership with effective corporate governance
Small-scale privatization	1	Little progress
	2	Substantial share privatized
	3	Comprehensive program almost ready for implementation
	4	Complete privatization of small companies with tradable ownership rights
	4+	Standards and performance typical of advanced industrial economies: no state ownership of small enterprises; effective tradability of land
Governance and enterprise restructuring	1	Soft budget constraints (lax credit and subsidy policies weakening financial discipline at the enterprise level); few other reforms to promote corporate governance
	2	Moderately tight credit and subsidy policy but weak enforcement of bankruptcy legislation and little action taken to strengthen competition and corporate governance
	3	Significant and sustained actions to harden budget constraints and to promote corporate governance effectively (e.g., privatization combined with tight credit and subsidy policies and/or enforcement of bankruptcy legislation)
	4	Substantial improvement in corporate governance (e.g.,, an account of an active corporate control market); significant new investment at the enterprise level
	4+	Standards and performance typical of advanced industrial economies: effective corporate control exercised through domestic financial institutions and markets, fostering market-driven restructuring
Price liberalization	1	Most prices formally controlled by the government.
	2	Price controls for several important product categories; state procurement at non-market prices remains substantial
	3	Substantial progress on price liberalization; state procurement at non-market prices largely phased out
	4	Comprehensive price liberalization; utility pricing reflects economic costs
	4+	Standards and performance typical of advanced industrial economies: comprehensive price liberalization; efficiency-enhancing regulation of utility pricing

Trade and foreign exchange system	1	Widespread import and/or export controls or very limited legitimate access to foreign exchange
	2	Some liberalization of import and/or export controls; almost full current account convertibility in principle but with a foreign exchange regime that is not fully transparent (possibly with multiple exchange rates)
	3	Removal of almost all quantitative and administrative import and export restrictions; almost full current account convertibility
	4	Removal of all quantitative and administrative import and export restrictions (apart from agriculture) and all significant export tariffs; insignificant direct involvement in exports and imports by ministries and state-owned trading companies; no major non uniformity of customs duties for non-agricultural goods and services; full and current account convertibility
	4+	Standards and performance norms of advanced industrial economies: removal of most tariff barriers; membership in WTO
Competition policy	1	No competition legislation and institutions.
	2	Competition policy legislation and institutions set up; some reduction of entry restrictions or enforcement action on dominant firms
	3	Some enforcement actions to reduce abuse of market power and to promote a competitive environment, including breakups of dominant conglomerates; substantial reduction of entry restrictions
	4	Significant enforcement actions to reduce abuse of market power and to promote a competitive environment
	4+	Standards and performance typical of advanced industrial economies: effective enforcement of competition policy; unrestricted entry to most markets
Banking reform and interest rate liberalization	1	Little progress beyond establishment of a two-tier system
	2	Significant liberalization of interest rates and credit allocation; limited use of directed credit or interest rate ceilings
	3	Substantial progress in establishment of bank solvency and of a framework for prudential supervision and regulation; full interest rate liberalization with little preferential access to cheap refinancing; significant lending to private enterprises and significant presence of private banks
	4	Significant movement of banking laws and regulations towards Bank of International Settlement (BIS) standards; well-functioning banking competition and effective prudential supervision; significant term lending to private enterprises; substantial financial deepening
	4+	Standards and performance norms of advanced industrial economies: full convergence of banking laws and regulations with BIS standards; provision of full set of competitive banking services

Securities markets and non-bank financial institutions	1	Little progress
	2	Formation of securities exchanges, market makers, and brokers; some trading in government paper and/or securities; rudimentary legal and regulatory framework for the issuance and trading of securities
	3	Substantial issuance of securities by private enterprises; establishment of independent share registries, secure clearance and settlement procedures, and some protection of minority shareholders; emergence of non-bank financial institutions (e.g. investment funds, private insurance and pension funds, leasing companies) and associated regulatory framework
	4	Securities laws and regulations approaching IOSCO standards; substantial market liquidity and capitalization; well-functioning non-bank financial institutions and effective regulation
	4+	Standards and performance norms of advanced industrial economies: full convergence of securities laws and regulations with IOSCO standards; fully developed non-bank intermediation

1 The classification system is simplified and expands on the judgment of the EBRD's Office of the Chief Economist. To refine further the classification system, pluses and minuses have been added to the 1–4 scale to indicate the borderline between two categories.

References

Buiter, Wilhelm, and Clemens Grafe. 2002. Anchor, float or abandon ship: Exchange rate regimes for the accession countries. Paper presented at the tenth anniversary conference of the EBRD, London (December 13-14).

Deutsche Bank Research. Key economic indicators: Bulgaria. Country infobase. http://www.dbresearch.com/servlet/reweb2.ReWEB?rwkey=u845&%24rwframe=0.

EBRD. *Transition report*. Various issues. London: EBRD.

EBRD. 2002. *Transition report 2002: Agriculture and rural transition*. London: EBRD.

EBRD. 2003a. *Country strategy for Bulgaria*. London: EBRD. http://www.ebrd.com/about/strategy/country/bulgaria/strategy.pdf.

EBRD. 2003b. *Transition report 2003: Integration and regional cooperation*. London: EBRD.

EBRD and World Bank. 1999. *Business environment and enterprise performance survey* (BEEPS). http://www.worldbank.org.ru/survey/front2.htm.

European Commission. 2003. *2003 Regular report on Bulgaria's progress towards accession*. Brussels.

Fries, Steven, Tatiana Lysenko, and Sasp Polanec. 2002. *Business environment and enterprise performance survey* (BEEPS). London: EBRD. http://www.ebrd.com/pubs/econ/workingp/84.pdf.

8 Macroeconomic Stability and Economic Growth

By Ilian Mihov, Associate Professor
of Economics, INSEAD

Edited and updated paper based on the conference[1]

The most notable fact about Bulgaria's economic performance is the impressive recovery in the years since the 1996-97 financial crises. From a macroeconomic point of view, Bulgaria has implemented a consistent set of policy reforms and institutional changes and has become a synonym for political and economic stability in the Balkans. This paper looks at the country's current economic performance and investigates the fundamental macroeconomic reasons for its success. It also provides a view toward the future: What are the policies and institutional changes that Bulgaria needs to undertake in order to ensure high rates of sustainable economic growth?

The main thrust of the paper is this key observation: There is a need to change the economic paradigm from a focus on direct policy intervention to a focus on creating the right economic environment. Instead of going after growth-promoting policies, we view the task of increasing growth rates in the country as a question of establishing the right environment for growth. Policy intervention still has a place in promoting economic growth. However, it should not be viewed as a direct intervention to augment growth factors like capital and labor, but rather an intervention that creates the incentives for physical and human capital accumulation.

The Current Situation

The Bulgarian economy grew at about 4.8 percent per year from 2001 to 2004, and the Economist Intelligence Unit expects 2005 growth to register at 5.7 percent (2005, 5). As a rate of growth sustained over a long period of time, this record is certainly commendable. Furthermore, given that the period was marred by several financial

1   I would like to thank Ivan Krastev for constructive discussions on the issues of economic and political development in Bulgaria. Research for this article was supported through the Blue Bird Project, which is financed by a consortium of international donors and administered by the Central European University. Specifically, contributions from the international donor Bank of Sweden Tercentenary Foundation were used to fund this work. The opinions expressed herein are the author's own and do not necessarily express the views of CEU or the Blue Bird Project. Correspondence: mihov@econ.insead.edu

Table 1. Growth rates in Bulgaria and selected countries

	GNI per capita in US$ at PPP	Growth 2000-02	2004 GNI per capita in US$ at PPP	Growth 2000-04
Bulgaria	6, 840	4.73%	7, 870	8.15%
Albania	4, 040	6.77%	5, 070	7.89%
Bosna and Herzegovina	5, 800	6.00%	7, 430	5.75%
Croatia	9, 760	3.97%	11,670	6.38%
Greece	18, 240	4.10%	22, 000	5.88%
Macedonia	6, 210	0.10%	6, 480	2.90%
Romania	6, 290	3.87%	8, 190	7.36%
Serbia	6, 380	5.17%		
Slovenia	17, 690	3.57%	20, 730	5.36%
Turkey	6, 120	2.57%	7, 680	4.93%
Area average	8, 737	4.09%	10, 350	5.98%
excluding Greece and Slovenia	6, 430	4.15%	7, 596	6.07%
EU average	24,900	2.03%	24,920	5.37%

Source: World Bank (2002 and 2005). Per capita GNI data is not available for Serbia after 2002. The ten countries that joined the EU in 2004 are not included in EU calculations for 2000-03.

crises in emerging markets and a global recession, the performance of the Bulgarian economy is certainly impressive. To understand why some policies work and why some policies fail, we start with a comparative analysis of economic growth in the period 2000-02 as well as the most recent data on gross national income, or GNI, per capita (measured at purchasing power parity exchange rates). Bulgaria performed quite well, when compared to the other countries from the Balkan region. Excluding the two industrialized countries from the region – Slovenia and Greece – the record of Bulgaria reveals both higher a GNI than the regional average and higher growth rate compared to all of the other countries in the region.

The question at this point is not so much how to generate growth – it is already happening. The key question is whether the current rate of growth is sustainable and more importantly whether it is sufficient to ensure political and social stability. The average annual growth rate for the region for 2000-02 (4.73 percent)[2] might be insufficient to generate the necessary social stability, since at this rate Bulgaria would catch up with the EU average after fifty years. Lifting the growth rate from 4.73 percent to 6 percent, which is a feasible increase for most countries, would reduce the period by one-third, to thirty-three years. This simple calculation shows that even small increases in growth rates can lead to dramatic changes in the economic well-being of the country in the long run. Furthermore, as a 2003 report by the Blue Bird Project argues, the 2000-02 growth rate did not generate public support for economic reforms. The report shows that while GDP had been steadily increasing in the country, the perception of the public was that economic welfare was deteriorating. The question is how long the public will put up with the current

---

2   The annual growth rate for Bulgaria for 2000-04 was a robust 8.15 percent.

reforms if the overwhelming majority perceives them as wrong-headed. The Blue Bird report argues that the government must implement support-enhancing policies in addition to growth-promoting policy changes. Here, a key ingredient of the support-enhancing policy is to create an environment where faster and more comprehensive economic growth can take place. This environment must provide incentives for everyone in the country to be a part of the growing economy. Whether the country has the right environment for sustainable growth depends on the drivers of economic growth.

What Drives Growth? The Role of Saving and Environmental Factors

Economic growth is a result of factor accumulation – human and physical capital – and of productivity improvements. The empirical and theoretical literature has identified many factors that promote growth, including macroeconomic stability, legal environment, political and social stability, taxation, competition, and trade. It is important, however, to keep in mind that most of these factors affect growth because they *create the environment for higher investment* (in physical or human capital).[3] Even more fundamentally, these factors affect saving – the willingness of consumers to forego current consumption for the sake of future consumption. In short, growth in poor countries is driven by investment, and saving finances investment. And of course, saving might take the form of physical or human capital.

In an open economy that allows for capital flows into and out of the country, local investment can be financed by foreign saving – this is the case for example with the much-desired foreign direct investment (FDI). Many policy discussions have been devoted to the issue of how to attract foreign investors and many observers have argued that in poor countries it is difficult to muster large savings pools that will finance investment. Historically this argument is largely incorrect. Most of the fast-growing economies have been growing by domestic saving and not foreign. Today, one of the fastest growing economies in the world is China, with an average growth rate over the past decade of about 10 percent per annum. In China, net foreign direct investment constitutes only about 15 percent of total investment. Domestic saving finances the remaining 85 percent of investment projects. China is poorer than Bulgaria, a fact that challenges the view that saving is a luxury to be done by rich countries. It is certainly worth pointing out that China is not an isolated case – the same is true for Singapore (throughout the decades of high growth)

---

3   Hall and Jones (1999) use the term "social infrastructure" to signify the economic environment linked to institutions and government policies. They argue that the social infrastructure explains not only differences in growth rates, but importantly also differences in the level of GDP per capita.

and for a transition economy such as Hungary. The lesson is that to grow fast an economy must exhibit high rates of domestic saving.

It is easy to draw the wrong lesson from this discussion. One might argue that if investment is the driver of the process of catching up with the rich countries, then the government could play a direct role by taxing at high rates and investing the funds by building factories. Clearly, that was the model of the socialist economies in the 1950s and 1960s. It is not necessary to expose the faults of this growth model, as they are well known. It is also not necessary to cite many examples of misguided investment in physical or human capital that failed to produce the expected high growth. But it is important to stress that the discussion of the link between saving, investment, and growth requires a more subtle interpretation: the role of governments is to *create the environment for high private saving rates*. Consumers will decide how much to save based on the rewards they receive from saving. This is the role of the governments in the region: to build the economic and political environment in a way that guarantees high returns for private investment. This is the engine of growth.

If saving is so important then how can the governments in the region increase saving rates? Two groups of policy and institutional reforms could be used to achieve this goal: 1) policies that are explicitly designed to raise the saving rate; or 2) policies and institutions that create the environment for high saving. As an example from the first group of reforms, one can point to various types of tax relief for saving. Such policies are implemented in many developed economies; in the US saving for retirement under certain conditions is exempted from taxation, and in most European countries income from various saving accounts is not taxable. The key point is that there are policies that can be directly targeted at improving the saving rate of the economy. But, of course, these policies are not the panacea – after all, the saved funds must bring in the necessary return to justify the sacrifice of consumption. And in this respect environmental factors play a bigger role.

The environmental factors are subtler and potentially more important because they create a transparent and coherent structure of incentives to save and invest. A list of such factors is:

- **Macroeconomic stability**. When inflation is rather stable and low, consumers are more willing to commit their funds to saving because they know that unexpected inflation will not erode their saving.
- **Political and social stability**. Rapid political and social changes create an environment of uncertainty and sharp policy shifts. Risk-averse consumers will be less willing to save under precarious political conditions.
- **Legal environment**. It is a simple truism to state that observance of property rights is fundamental for saving. The fear of expropriation leads to low rates of saving.

- **Financial stability**. The banking sector plays a key role in channeling saving into productive uses. If the banking system is unstable, consumers will shy away from putting their money in banks and there will be fewer funds to be loaned. Investment will go down and with it the rate of economic growth.

We can view the rate of saving in Bulgaria in comparison to other countries in the process of catching up (not, of course, in comparison to the United States or other developed nations). Despite the recent progress in stabilizing the economic and political environment, saving is still very low in Bulgaria. While such other countries in transition as the Czech Republic and Hungary have managed to sustain a saving rate of over 20 percent, saving rates in Bulgaria have fluctuated between 8 and 15 percent. Again, the rate of saving depends on many behavioral characteristics but it is not necessarily determined by the wealth of the nation – remembering that China, poorer than Bulgaria or for that matter than any of the Southeast European economies, has a saving rate three times higher than the average for the region. Clearly a large part of the discrepancy between saving in the fast-growing Asian economies and the Southeast European countries can be explained by "cultural factors," but there is certainly room for policy intervention. Saving does respond to incentives, and when the economic environment is right saving will also increase in Bulgaria.

Why did former communist countries change from the high saving regime in place before 1989 to a regime of negligible saving rates? Certainly to a large extent

Table 2. Domestic saving as % GDP

	Domestic Saving 2000	Domestic Saving 2003
Bulgaria	**10.97%**	**11.97%**
Albania	-2.90%	2.21%
Bosna and Herzegovina	-10.30%	-14.04%
Croatia	16.37%	20.66%
Greece	13.86%	18.00%
Macedonia	-0.41%	3.44%
Romania	13.63%	15.31%
Serbia	-4.46%	-5.20%
Slovenia	24.24%	25.21%
Turkey	16.78%	19.68%
Central European economies		
Czech Republic	25.98%	25.38%
Hungary	26.49%	22.14%
Poland	19.58%	14.99%
Some fast-growing economies		
China	39.94%	46.95%
Korea	31.44%	31.91%
Singapore	49.76%	46.69%

Source: World Bank (2002 and 2005)

the difference is explained by the fact that saving before 1989 was largely involuntary. But from a policy point of view a more important reason is the macroeconomic and financial instability that followed 1989: high inflation rates and sequences of banking crises melted away the savings of the general public. In such an environment of instability and uncertainty saving seems undesirable.

Macroeconomic Stability: The Role of Fiscal Policy

It follows from the previous discussion that an important factor in raising saving rates is economic stability. To begin, it is important to consider fiscal policy as a determinant of macroeconomic stability. Bulgarian governments have been quite prudent in recent years with budget deficits in the range between 0 and 1 percent. One way to secure the achievements on the fiscal policy front is to constrain policy makers to behave within a framework that guarantees stability. However, imposing such constraints is quite complicated. Quantitative restrictions – like the 3 percent limit on the deficit in the EU's Stability and Growth Pact – do not necessarily work either because they restrict policy too much at the wrong time, or because violations of such rules are difficult to punish. Instead of quantitative restrictions, a recent paper argued that fiscal policy should be constrained by checks and balances (Fatás and Mihov 2003). Lack of checks and balances makes it possible to use fiscal policy for opportunistic reasons. Frequent exercise of fiscal policy creates macroeconomic volatility and overall instability. One potential link between the institutional structure of the country and economic growth can be represented schematically as follows:

More political constraints => Lower variability of fiscal policy =>
Lower macroeconomic instability => More saving => Higher growth

What are the political constraints that are to be imposed? The goal is to reduce the power of the executive branch to use spending and taxation in an opportunistic manner, for example for the purpose of improving an incumbent's chances for reelection. The empirical evidence shows clearly that countries with more veto points on the executive's decision-making power have more stable fiscal policies. There are various ways of increasing the checks and balances in the country, for example through an independent judiciary that can challenge decisions of the government, or with a budgetary process that will allow the legislature to curb the power of the executive branch. Of course, the latter is meaningful only if the executive and the legislature have different sources of legitimacy. If governments are simply appointed by the parliament, then it is difficult to argue that the legislature will veto the executive's decisions.

Table 3. Political constraints

Country	Political Constraints
Bulgaria	**0.74**
Average	0.38
Albania	0.52
Greece	0.70
Romania	0.56
Turkey	0.62
Serbia and Montenegro	0.46
Bosnia and Herzegovina	0.00
Croatia	--
FYR Macedonia	0.41
Slovenia	0.73

Source: Henisz (2000)

Where does Bulgaria stand in the ranking of political constraints? One measure of veto points is constructed by Henisz (2000) and reported in table 3, below. The index ranges from 0 (no constraints) to 1 (all possible constraints: independently elected executive with a bicameral parliament, an independent judiciary, and a federal structure). The index also adjusts for the political alignment across branches (for example, if the executive and the parliament are from the same party, then the likelihood of vetoing a decision can be expected to be lower). Interestingly, Bulgaria scores quite high with an index of 0.74. This is close to the indices of the more developed economies (where the index is usually between 0.75 and 0.85).

Overall, macroeconomic stability can be an outcome of policy conducted in a discretionary way or the result of an institutional arrangement that restricts policy makers in certain ways. The institutional solution – by separation of powers in the case of fiscal policy or by having an explicit monetary target in the case of monetary policy – seems to provide a better environment for long-term strategic planning by consumers and firms.

Monetary Stability: The Pros and Cons of Early "Euroization"

Monetary stability is manifested in low and stable inflation rates. High and variable inflation rates have several negative effects on the economy. First and foremost, they complicate decision making by individuals by making nominal returns highly volatile. This complication naturally inhibits saving and investment in the country. Furthermore, recent research has shown that high inflation is one of the most important factors in increasing economic inequality in the transition economies (Ivaschenko 2003).

Bulgaria lived through the perils of monetary irresponsibility in the first half of the 1990s. The country has also seen the ghost of hyperinflation, and the public has a very good sense of how high inflation can damage the economy. Bulgaria's record from 1990 to 1997 reveals that its policy makers cannot manage monetary policy in a reasonable way. Therefore, the adoption of a monetary regime with an explicit target in the form of a currency board was a very desirable development. The currency board brought an immediate reduction in policy volatility, and this reduction is important for at least two reasons: 1) more stability as argued above leads to higher saving (investment) rates, and 2) macroeconomic stability reduces economic inequality.

The success of the currency board in Bulgaria in securing stability is indisputable. Recently, however, several researchers have argued that Bulgaria should go further and adopt the euro as its currency. This argument has also been advanced for other EU accession countries (Buiter and Grafe 2002; Bratkowski and Rostowski 2002). Is there a case to be made for or against "euroization"? Before entering this debate let's define "early euroization." It is the adoption of the euro as a national currency *with* the consent of the European Central Bank (ECB), but *without* necessarily participating in the ECB council as a voting member. It is certainly possible also to adopt the euro *without* the consent of the ECB; this is referred to as "unilateral euroization."

The key argument against giving up national monetary independence is that the country loses monetary policy as a tool for stabilization of the economy. But Bulgaria has a currency board arrangement already. A currency board requires that active monetary policy be relinquished. Critics of euroization often argue that a poor country like Bulgaria needs monetary policy as a stabilization and growth-enhancing tool. These criticisms fail to make the argument from an economic point of view because they argue that in general, discretion (possibly with some constraints) is better than a rule (of the euroization type). Economists usually make their arguments using the marginal impact of the proposed institutional change. And the marginal difference here is between a currency board and euroization, and not between unconstrained monetary policy and euroization. Bulgaria already does not have access to monetary policy as an active tool for macroeconomic management. When left without any restrictions, monetary policy can be very powerful and important in ensuring macroeconomic stability. Unfortunately, Bulgaria's historical record shows that monetary policy can be easily abused. Hence the country is better off without discretionary monetary policy. Then the question is, what is the difference between euroization and the currency board? In terms of loss of monetary policy as a tool, there is simply no difference.

The Bulgarian currency board is not a plain vanilla board and it is argued that monetary policy can still be conducted via the fiscal accounts on the balance sheet of the issue department. It is possible that such policy intervention is beneficial, but it is equally possible that it is highly damaging for the economy. Many scientific papers have shown that unchecked policy interventions conducted by the government (not the central bank) can be quite damaging for the economy. Thus, it seems that the possibility of having an active monetary policy in a currency board setting is an argument for restricting further the monetary authority (by euroization, for example) rather than an argument to preserve the current arrangement.

Should the euro be adopted unilaterally? It should not. Although theoretically unilateral euroization might still be preferable to a currency board, from a practical point of view unilateral euroization can lead to undesirable outcomes. In particular, the ECB council and the European Commission are against unilateral euroization and therefore unilateral euroization can antagonize these institutions and cause problems on the way to accession. Thus the undesirable outcomes may arise from the political rather than the economic sphere.

Why is the ECB against euroization? The official argument is that unilateral euroization is against the letter of the EU treaty, namely the "conversion rate" between the national currency and the euro is a matter of common interest and must be determined jointly by the EU countries and the accession country. This argument is correct, and countries with currency board arrangements should consider early (negotiated) euroization as opposed to unilateral euroization. A potentially more serious – unofficial – argument is that the ECB council does not want to be in charge of a country that is not a member of the EU. Such a view can certainly be rationalized from the individual viewpoint of the policy maker, but not from a social welfare perspective.

How to proceed with *early* euroization? If the negotiations between Bulgaria and the EU go as planned, Bulgaria will become a member in 2007. At that time Bulgaria, unlike the UK, will not have the choice of opting out of economic and monetary union (EMU). This means that *the euro will become* Bulgaria's currency anyway. At the time when Bulgaria becomes a member of the EMU, it will enter into a number of relationships with the ECB: it will have a representative in the decision-making body (the ECB Council), and the Bulgarian National Bank will have certain obligations as part of the European system of central banks. Early euroization is the negotiated (with the ECB and the European Commission) adoption of the euro before Bulgaria enters EMU. It should be viewed as preparation, or as part of the process of becoming a member of the EMU and not as a unilateral move. An often posed question is, "Why not wait?" One good answer is, "Why wait?" The proponents of EMU have made the argument that a monetary union brings many benefits to the member countries, benefits that largely offset the loss of national monetary policy. If one buys this argument – and presumably one day the accession country must buy it – then why not have these benefits earlier rather than later? To make the argument for waiting, one has to argue that from the currency board to the EMU Bulgaria will go through a transitional period that involves active monetary policy. This argument has one big flaw: it is a prescription for a financial crisis, as one would anticipate the local currency to depreciate. Such expectations when they become widespread also become self-fulfilling. After all, the transition between the currency board and the euro may involve active monetary policy but the point is that such transition can be very costly and the proponents of waiting must provide a very clear theoretical justification for the need for a transitional period. At this time no one has made a credible argument about the nature of this transition and the feasibility of such process.

What about the seigniorage?[4] Currently the central bank gets income by keeping income-earning securities on its asset side. With euroization, this income will disappear, as the European Central Bank will issue all notes. Is this a serious cost? There are two components in the answer. First, if euroization is negotiated Bulgaria can receive its part of the seigniorage as part of the deal. There are technical problems, but they can be resolved easily (notice that there is already distribution for seigniorage in the EMU). Second, people closely associated with the Ministry of Finance whose goal is to balance the budget usually make the seigniorage argument. For economists, the budget is not a goal but an instrument of policy. The ultimate goal is economic welfare. The economic argument is that increased trade, increased transparency, elimination of exchange rate risk, reduction of transaction costs – benefits associated with euroization – will more than outweigh the loss of seigniorage even if the ECB does not distribute the part of the seigniorage to those who adopt the euro early.

According to Rose (2001) having a currency union increases trade (with the other euro countries) by a factor of 3 relative to using different currencies. Admittedly this number is very high and probably will not apply to Bulgaria, but even a simple increase of trade by 30 percent to 50 percent will be highly beneficial for these economies. Frankel and Romer (1999) argue that an increase of trade-to-GDP ratio by one percentage point increases GDP per capita by more than 1.5 percent. Admittedly, these improvements are large and the experience of Bulgaria might differ from these projections. But even if the benefits are only 50 percent of these estimates, the country will add the much-needed extra percentage point to its growth and accelerate the process of catching up with the wealthy countries in the EU.

---

4   Seigniorage is the profit that results from the difference in the cost of printing money and the face value of that money.

Overall, it is hard to find a serious *economic* argument against an early transition from a currency board to the euro. The benefits of euroization are also difficult to quantify and hence it is hard to make a strong case for early euroization. Nonetheless, it is important to use the correct arguments when discussing the option of early euroization, and "losing monetary policy as an active tool" does not seem to be a correct argument for a country with a currency board arrangement.

Summing up: What Must Change to Improve Growth Prospects?

Changes in economic institutions and economic policies designed to improve the economic welfare in Bulgaria must be based on the fundamental belief that growth is by and large a result of private initiative. Market failures do have important consequences for economic development, and governments can play a role in addressing these market failures. But the lesson that growth economics has learned (and is still learning) from the past forty years is that the direct policy intervention of raising the process of capital or labor accumulation does not work. Growth-enhancing policies are subtle and indirect – they must create stability and promote private initiative. The role of the government is to create stability (via fiscal and monetary policy) and to set the incentives for private initiative. Macroeconomic stability, efficient legal environment, social cohesion, these are the ingredients that make economic actors change their perspective from a short-term view to long-term strategies. These long-term strategies of saving and investing in human and physical capital produce sustainable long-term growth.

References

Blue Bird Project. 2003. Getting incentives right, getting perceptions right. Center for Liberal Strategies, Sofia.

Bratkowski, Andrej, and Jacek Rostowski. 2002. Why unilateral euroization makes sense for (some) accession countries. Manuscript.

Buiter, Willem, and Clemens Grafe. 2002. Anchor, float or abandon ship: Exchange rate regimes for the accession countries. Paper presented at the tenth anniversary conference of the EBRD, London (December 13-14).

Economist Intelligence Unit. 2005. *Country Report: Bulgaria* (October).

Fatás, Antonio, and Ilian Mihov. 2002. The case for restricting fiscal policy discretion. CEPR Discussion Paper 3277, Centre for Economic Policy Research, London.

——— 2003. The case for restricting fiscal policy discretion. *Quarterly Journal of Economics* (November).

Frankel, Jeffrey, and David Romer. 1999. Does trade cause growth? *American Economic Review* 89 (June).

Hall, Robert, and Charles Jones. 1999. Why do some countries produce so much more output per worker than others? *Quarterly Journal of Economics* (February).

Henisz, Witold J. 2000. The institutional environment for economic growth. *Economics and Politics* 12: 1-31.

Ivaschenko, Oleksiy. 2003. Growth and inequality: Evidence from transitional economies in the 1990s. In *Inequality and growth: Theory and applications*, ed. Theo Eicher and Stephen Turnovsky. Cambridge, Mass.: MIT Press.

Rose, Andrew. 2001. One money, one market: The effect of common currencies on trade. *Economic Policy* 30 (April): 7-33.

World Bank. 2002. *World development indicators 2002*. World Bank Publications.

———. 2005. *World development indicators 2005*. World Bank Publications.

9 Bulgaria in a Longer-term Perspective: The Risk Associated with the Pension System

Krassen Stanchev, PhD, Director of the
Institute for Market Economics

Edited and updated paper based on the conference

External developments pose little risk to the Bulgarian economy, and the worst period of adjustment and reorientation is over. The first part of this paper attempts to provide some reasoning that supports this conviction. However, issues do remain that have not received proper attention because of their longer-term nature as economic phenomena. One of these issues, perhaps the most urgent, is the deficiency of the existing pension system. The second half of this discussion summarizes the worries that come from the analysis of this issue by the Institute for Market Economics (IME).

Resilience to External Shocks

A quick overview of Bulgaria's performance in the 1990s will reveal that its economy has become resilient to external shocks. The country has successfully weathered a number of such shocks, namely the global financial crisis of the mid-1990s, the Russia crisis of 1998, the shock related to the Kosovo war of 1999, the petroleum price hikes in recent years, and the depreciation of the euro against the U.S. dollar.[1]

Different factors have contributed to this relative robustness. Obviously, the underdevelopment of domestic capital markets helped the Bulgarian economy avoid global turbulence. On the other hand, structural reforms, which rebounded in 1997-98, contributed to the flexibility that made export rerouting possible in 1999 and increased energy efficiency after 1997.

An additional factor was the successful re-channeling of Bulgaria's foreign trade, from more than 50 percent of exports going to COMECOM countries in 1989-90 to more than 50 percent going to the EU in the late 1990s. Thanks to some legacies of the mid-1980s and to the uneven success of reforms from 1990-97, this re-channeling took place over a relatively long period of time. At the same time, Bulgaria is by no

---

1   It is still questionable whether the events of September 11, 2001, and the war on terrorism will have a major negative influence on Bulgaria's attractiveness to foreign direct investment. Thus far the evidence is mixed and the overall slowdown in 2001 and 2002 is difficult to attribute to the isolated impact of 9/11.

means isolated. The slowdown in the EU and the crisis in Turkey[2] decelerated growth from 5.4 percent in 2000 to 4.1 percent in 2001 and widened the current account deficit to over 7 percent of GDP (up from 6 percent in 2000). Real GDP growth was 4.9 percent in 2002, 4.5 percent in 2003, and 5.6 percent in 2004. The current account deficits for 2002 and 2003 were, respectively, 5.3 percent and 8.4 percent. The 2004 deficit was 7.5 percent (Deutsche Bank Research).

Aside from these constellations, the consensus GDP growth forecasts for Bulgaria in 2002 were higher than those of all other EU accession countries except Romania, which recovered from a sharp contraction in 1997-99.[3] Deutsche Bank Research's 2005 GDP growth forecast for Bulgaria (4.8 percent) is slightly less than those for Turkey (5 percent) and Romania (5.5 percent), two other EU candidate countries. However, Bulgaria's forecast was greater than Croatia's (3.8 percent), another candidate country (Deutsche Bank Research).

Recent Background

The average budget deficit for the period 1991-96 (the first years of transition) was 6.9 percent of GDP. In comparison, after the establishment of the currency board, the deficit declined to 0.9 percent.

Average inflation between 1991 and 1997 was about 240 percent, while the average decrease in the GDP equaled 4.9 percent. The years following the introduction of the currency board witnessed an average 4 percent increase in GDP and inflation of 5.85 percent, while the inflation tax amounted to the following: 1.6 percent in 1998, 7 percent in 1999, 11.3 percent in 2000, 4.8 percent in 2001, 3.8 percent in 2002, 5.6 percent in 2003, and 4 percent in 2004.

Another factor revealing the increase in government redistribution abilities is related to the dynamics of government debt. Its domestic equivalent in 1991 was 13 percent of GDP while in 1996 it climbed to 60 percent of GDP. The dynamics of the external debt are even more telling: 168 percent in 1991, 127 percent in 1992, 109 percent in 1993, 129 percent in 1994, and 242 percent in 1995. In contrast, the internal debt for 2002 was 6 percent of GDP and the external debt was 72 percent of GDP. In 2004, external debt was 70 percent of GDP.

Current Constellations

On the external side, it is virtually impossible for Bulgaria to change its economic orientation. Although there will be an attempt for greater Russian involvement in

---

2   Together the EU and Turkey account for 60 percent of Bulgaria's exports.
3   See EBRD (2002, 5, 17). See also JP Morgan (2002) and Deutsche Bank (2002, 3).

some sectors, like nuclear power, the years for external adjustment are over and the country is already a part of the EU economic space.

Current constellations are either neutral or rather beneficial. For one, the 9/11 events did not have a negative effect on the two most important sectors of the Bulgarian economy, tourism and transport. The estimated annual growth rate of tourism for 2000–05 is 10 percent. In 2003, the number of tourists visiting Bulgaria increased by 18 percent, and the total number of tourists visiting during 2004 increased by 14 percent (National Statistical Institute). Thus, growth figures for 2004 will likely be aggressive as well (Republic of Bulgaria). Second, Bulgaria has grown relatively quickly irrespective of the recession/slowdown in external demand, notably from the EU and Turkey. Third, there is no probable development in the neighboring Balkans that would significantly divert Bulgaria's economic performance. Finally, the country seems well positioned to weather euro-U.S. dollar exchange rate fluctuations, from both a debt management point of view and a real-economy point of view.

On the domestic side, the risks are few. The business environment seems either to have improved or to be developing in the right direction, although there are differences between tax and quasi-tax segments. The effective corporate income tax rate in 2002 was 23.5 percent, a lower percentage than that produced by the first-wave EU accession economies. The effective personal income tax rate is 12.8 percent, which is also lower than the average (hopeful) EU accession level. The policy commitment is first to lower the rates further and second to make them flatter. The quasi-tax burden, however, is significant: the cost of compliance and the cost of dealing with the government were expected to be as high as 12 percent of GDP in 2001 and 2002 (see Stanchev, Gancheva, and Stoev 2000). There is a move toward simplifying the entry barriers and ensuring more reliable contract enforcement procedures.

If there are any risks, they are related to government policies. One area to look into is the scope of government involvement in managing state-owned enterprises used as venues for cross-subsidies and, more rarely, "social" policies (see Stanchev and Stoev 2002). The other area is an area of domestic debt related to the deficits of the pay-as-you-go pension system and to municipal debts. These two problems are difficult to tackle because the incumbent government risked election promises to increase both. Today, any reasonable approach could damage the government's public image and result in confidence losses. Municipal debts are hardly regulated. For this reason it is difficult to obtain reliable information. It is clear, however, that these debts increase by an average of 0.2 percent of GDP per annum, at a conservative estimate. A more significant issue is the deficit of the quasi-government pension fund: it grows by an estimated average of 0.8 percent of GDP per annum. The government vision does not allow for a sustainable solution; at best, judging from what has been communicated, it may reduce the annual increase somewhat – perhaps by half –by reducing the available income by 3.5 percent.

Systemic Risks of the Existing Pay-as-you-go Model

The National Social Security Institute (NSI) generates a deficit (about LV0.9 billion for 2002) covered by the government. The deficit of NSI pension funds increased from LV140 million in 2000 to LV442 million in 2001, and further to LV889 million in 2002. In 2003, the deficit in the state pension insurance fund was LV253 million, although it was forecasted to reach LV382 million (Ivanova 2004). However, the deficit in 2004 increased to LV576 million (Mitreva 2004). The present model of social security contributions generates gaps between revenues and expenditures that the government will eventually not be able to bridge.[4]

For demographic reasons, fewer and fewer people will be entering the system. The alternative private pillar is eleven times smaller than the pay-as-you-go system. There is no incentive for those who pay social security contributions to choose a level higher than the minimum wage. That is, those who pay more do not receive more benefits; rather, everyone is guaranteed a pension within a small range of possible outcomes. The people are not motivated to allocate a greater share of their present income for future consumption.

The pay-as-you-go model is based on the so-called solidarity principle. However, solidarity can hardly exist when the number of those who give is smaller than the number of those who get. Usually, the principle of solidarity works when the majority in a society generates income and pays while a smaller group of people in need receive some kind of assistance.

Given the currency board, the only way the government can cover additional expenditures is through an increased tax burden. Monetary financing cannot be used to decrease the real level of expenditures through inflation. Thus, it is reasonable to expect constantly increasing subsidies for the NSI via debts and taxes. The room to maneuver is narrowing. The government's ability to react is significantly limited by its generous promises and rhetoric and by the fact that most of the players, including international financial institutions, were involved in choosing the present system in 1998-99.

Instead of Conclusion

Given the expected increase in budget expenditures related to the reform of the army according to the standards of NATO, to the implementation of environmental commitments – including the respective EU *acquis* and international agreements already signed – as well as to the recently announced plan to build a nuclear power

---

4   To make clear the character of the problem, it suffices to mention that the deficit of the National Social Security Institute equals 1.5 times the expected government revenues for 2002 from the income tax (about LV557 million). A substantial increase in the deficit is quite possible in the years to come.

plant in Belene, the ability of the budget to meet additional expenditures will be extremely limited.

The table below summarizes the provisional costs of already declared government priorities, including construction of the nuclear power plant and other systemic risk burdens but excluding the provisional rise of municipal debts, which is tackled every year on an ad hoc basis.

Table 1. Government priorities and related expenditures for 2002-05 (in $ million)

	2002	2003	2004	2005
GDP	14040	14601.6	15185.66	15793.1
Provisional expenditures				
1. Foreign debt payments	1303.7	1328.7	1353.7	1378.7
2. Environmental protection expenditures (with respect to EU compliance requirements)	1265	1265	1265	1265
3. Expenditures related to NATO accession (3% of GDP)	421.2	438	455.6	473.8
4. Deficit of the state pension fund	200	200	200	200
Additional expenditures				
Additional expenditures if building the nuclear plant in Belene	215	215	215	215
Total	3404.9	3446.7	3489.3	3532.5
Expenditures/GDP in %	24.3	23.6	23	22.4
Tax revenues (central government budget) as a % of GDP	31.6	32	32	32

Source: National statistics, Ministry of Finance, IME estimates and forecast

References

Deutsche Bank. 2002. Global markets research (July 2).

Deutsche Bank Research. Key economic indicators: Bulgaria. Country infobase. http://www. dbresearch.de/servlet/reweb2.ReWEB?rwkey=u1562080&%24rwframe=0 (September 2005).

EBRD. 2002. Transition report update (May).

Mitreva, Hristina. 2004. Report about the execution of the state social security budget for year 2004. National Social Security Institute. http://www.noi.bg/en/index.html.

Ivanova, Gergana. 2004. Social insurance revenues exceed target by BGN 450M. Global News Wire – Asia Africa Intelligence Wire (January 7).

JP Morgan. 2002. *Central & Eastern Europe, Middle East & Africa Weekly,* July 12, 2.

National Statistical Institute. http://www.nsi.bg/Index_e.htm.

Republic of Bulgaria. National Statistical Institute. Social statistics: Tourism, http://www.nsi. bg/SocialActivities_e/Tourism_e.htm.

Stanchev, Krassen, Yordanka Gancheva, and George Stoev. 2000. Private companies' costs of dealing with the government (a survey on Bulgaria) [in Bulgarian]. http://www.ime-bg.org/en/index.htm

Stanchev, Krassen, and George Stoev. 2002. Government activism is back in fashion. *IME Monthly Review* [in Bulgarian] (June). http://www.ime-bg.org/en/index.htm.

Economic Reform: From Stabilization to Growth

Alfred Schipke, Lecturer in Public Policy, John F. Kennedy School of Government, Harvard University

Edited and updated paper based on the conference

Although I would not consider myself to be an expert on economic issues particularly unique to Bulgaria, I have quite a bit of experience when it comes to countries with a currency board arrangement. At the end of 2001, I was involved in trying to find a solution for Argentina and discussed several policy options with both the government and the representatives of the banking sector. More relevant for Bulgaria, however, are the insights I have gained from my work with Estonia. Estonia is, of course, another transition economy that has had a currency board arrangement pegged to the euro; Estonia joined the EU in 2004 and is expected to join Europe's economic and monetary union (EMU) in 2006.

This discussion focuses on macroeconomic aspects of Bulgarian reform. Bulgaria made substantial strides over the last couple of years in terms of its macroeconomic management, which are worth reviewing. However, it is more productive to focus on the vulnerabilities and challenges that still lie ahead. Nevertheless, one has to give the current administration credit for coming a long way in reestablishing macroeconomic stability and therefore setting the foundation for sustainable growth and an improvement in the standard of living.

This paper begins with a snapshot of Bulgaria's current economic performance and brief comments on privatization and FDI investments. Before moving on to issues related to the currency board arrangement in the context of EU accession, the paper briefly mentions how the latest external developments might cause vulnerabilities for Bulgaria.

Macroeconomic Developments

Growth and Unemployment. Bulgaria's economy operated near its long-term growth potential in 2000, but economic activity slowed somewhat from 2001 onward. The economy has, however, shown substantial resilience despite the sluggishness of economic activity in other parts of Europe. With respect to Bulgaria's current growth performance, the country is similar to the Baltic states. However, while most analysts and the government still assumed that growth would be strong in 2002-03, the external environment was deteriorating, and the country still faced a persistently high rate of unemployment amounting to almost 20 percent. Since then, unemployment has dropped and growth for 2005 is projected to be strong. The unemployment rate stood at 10 percent for the second quarter of 2005, which is a significant improvement from the 19.4 percent rate of mid-2001.

Fiscal Position. A key accomplishment has been the government's ability to reduce and maintain a relatively low fiscal deficit; from 1999-2002, the deficit hovered at around 1 percent of GDP. In 2003, the budget was in balance, and in 2004 the government registered a fiscal surplus of 1.8 percent (Deutsche Bank Research). Given Bulgaria's currency board arrangement, though, fiscal policy remains the only short-term instrument and therefore Bulgaria did not take advantage of the 1998-2003 period to generate surpluses, which would have given the country a higher degree of freedom and would have reduced potential vulnerabilities. The objective of the government to reach a balanced budget by 2005 might not be sufficiently ambitious in light of the challenges that lie ahead.

Monetary and Credit Conditions. Monetary and credit aggregates grew rather rapidly in 2000-02 – again a phenomenon that we can observe in other transition economies with a currency board arrangement. There is, of course, substantial scope for re-monetization. Hence, Bulgaria can afford to have stronger liquidity growth while the impact on prices in the non-tradable sector is likely to remain subdued. However, credit growth in 2002 was extremely strong. Part of this can be explained through the introduction of the euro as a currency. In the process of exchanging national European currencies for new euros, people ended up depositing the funds in the banking sector, part of which found itself as credit to the domestic currency. This process is, of course, likely to be a one-time phenomenon. More worrisome – especially from a financing perspective – is the fact that credit to households has been rising substantially. Lending to households was growing at year-on-year rates of over 75 percent in October 2004, while lending to non-financial corporations was rising at a 40 percent rate. Credit growth was also robust in 2005; lending to households was growing at year-on-year rates of over 80 percent in March and April 2005, but fell to less than 70 percent in July. Lending to non-financial corporations, which accounts for nearly two-thirds of total domestic credit, was rising at approximately a 25 percent rate in July and August.

Inflation. On the inflation front, the performance has not been as impressive and inflation continues to be substantially higher than in the euro zone, with the corresponding result of an appreciation of the CPI-based real effective exchange rate. Especially in 2002, inflation was higher than expected. While this might merely reflect the impact of an increase in indirect taxes and a hike in administrative prices, even an adjusted inflation rate would still be higher than inflation in the euro zone. While this positive inflation differential might not necessarily have adverse implications for Bulgaria's competitiveness, it might cause some problems in the run-up to EMU.

Current Account Deficit. The most obvious vulnerability stems from the current account deficit. Countries with large productive gains should, of course, be in a position to sustain sizeable current account deficits and, in principle, a current account deficit of some 5 percent to 6 percent does not necessarily have to be seen as being too large. However, the current account deficit rose from 5.6 percent in 2002 to 8.4 percent in 2003, and in 2004 it reached 7.5 percent of GDP (Deutsche Bank Research). The breakout for the current account balance for the third quarter of 2004 showed that deficit in goods trade worsened from the same period in 2003, but this shortfall was more than made up by surpluses in services trade and by increases in remittances from Bulgarians working abroad. For the second quarter of 2005, the deficit in goods trade worsened compared with the second quarter of 2004, but the fall in the services surplus and the rise in the deficit on investment income over the corresponding period were much less pronounced. The current account deficit is financed mostly through a combination of FDI and bank borrowing.

Privatization. One issue of particular interest is the macroeconomics of privatization. But there are a couple of issues that are quite worrisome from the point of view of FDI inflows, productivity increases, and sources of future economic growth. First, as the example of the deal for the Bulgarian tobacco company demonstrates, sales of enterprises in this country still have substantial restrictions attached, such as the employment commitments that future owners have to make. While it was understandable that a government with an unemployment rate of almost 20 percent in 2001 (based on an unemployment survey) tried to minimize the adverse labor market impacts of privatization, this ultimately delayed the adjustment process. Here it would be preferable to provide direct support to those who are being laid off, which in turn could be financed through higher sales prices.

Second, and more importantly, as the privatization process is slowly coming to an end in both the financial and the industrial sector, the attraction of FDI might be hampered and the productivity gains be less pronounced. Some of the productivity gains that Bulgaria experienced early in this decade were related to increases in efficiency due to the restructuring process. Once this comes to an end, productivity gains have to come from other sources and would require for example a vibrant entrepreneurial class. However, given not only the current business environment but also the lending strategies of the financial sector and the lack of developed domestic money and capital markets, it is questionable whether the country will be able to sustain the inflows of past levels, especially in the form of non-debt creating inflows. The efforts underway (and potentially supported by a World Bank loan) are commendable in that they address such key issues as completing the privatization process, improving the legal and regulatory framework with respect to business activities, making labor markets more flexible and expanding the social safety net.

But even if all of these reforms are implemented on time, and there are doubts as to how quickly they can be implemented because of political economy considerations and the opposition by labor unions, it usually takes some time before such legislative measures actually lead to a change in behavior. Time, however, is of the essence. Given the straitjacket of a currency board arrangement, Bulgaria's external debt stock, and the large current account deficit, Bulgaria is dependent on large capital inflows. Although many would argue that the experience from Argentina is not relevant for Bulgaria, it does reveal one key element in that the introduction of a currency board arrangement is similar to a time inconsistency problem: the introduction of a currency board arrangement is similar to a commitment of the government. However, the implementation of the measures (structural policies such as privatization, the creation of a vibrant private sector, and labor market flexibility) that ensure that the currency board arrangement is actually credible at all times even during a period of external shocks takes many years and is certainly not yet completed in Bulgaria.

Vulnerabilities of Economic Growth in the Short to Medium Term. What kind of vulnerabilities might Bulgaria face? The devaluations of the Brazilian real in early 1999 and the Turkish lira in early 2001 were potentially worrisome for any emerging market with a relatively high stock of external debt, a large current account deficit, and a fixed exchange rate system. While today financial markets seem to distinguish more clearly between strong and weaker performers – thereby reducing the likelihood of contagion – a prolonged crisis in Turkey and Brazil would have increased the cost of financing for Bulgaria as well. Fortunately, neither crisis was particularly prolonged. Following a drop of 7.5 percent in 2001, Turkey's real GDP grew by 7.9 percent in 2002, 5.8 percent in 2003, and 8.4 percent in 2004. Still, given the proximity of Turkey and the fact that Turkey is one of Bulgaria's main trading partners, a slowdown in economic activity or even another recession combined with a further depreciation of the exchange rate would have real adverse implications for Bulgaria.

What about the Global Environment?

Recent developments in the United States, for example, are also hardly encouraging. A drop in retail sales and continued skepticism on the part of investors, compounded by accounting scandals that are not likely to disappear any time soon, are likely to have an adverse impact on the recovery. More importantly though is the fact that some indicators seem to suggest that there has been a structural shift with respect to the dollar-euro exchange rate and a further depreciation of the U.S. dollar is quite likely. The public announcement by the managing director of the IMF that under such circumstances a coordinated intervention is warranted recently raised the concern for a somewhat disorderly adjustment. Of course, in the short term, Bulgaria is likely to profit from a weaker dollar in terms of its U.S.-dollar-denominated debt service obligations. However, a delayed U.S. recovery combined with a substantial depreciation of the U.S. currency is likely to affect Europe and especially its export sector. This, of course, would mean bad news for Bulgaria as well.

Currency Board and Exit Strategy

Given the continued uncertainties that exist in international markets, the controversy must be addressed regarding whether countries that have adopted a currency board, maintained the currency board arrangement for some time, and have a clear exit strategy in terms of EMU membership should not wait to adopt the euro but instead adopt it unilaterally. This question is not so much directed at potential accession countries but at the European Central Bank (ECB). Countries that have successfully managed within the confines (or straitjacket) of a currency board and intend to adopt the euro at some point should consider whether, from a cost-benefit analysis, adopting the euro unilaterally would speed up the convergence process and induce even more confidence by, for example, eliminating the remaining foreign exchange risk. Adopting the euro unilaterally would also demonstrate to all market participants the need to speed up structural reforms. Bulgaria and some other countries might come to the conclusion that such a switch would be beneficial.

However, the ECB has basically blocked a discussion of the pros and cons for the various countries. In private and public the ECB has indicated that accession countries "cannot" unilaterally adopt the euro. A colleague at the Kennedy School raised such a question at the ECB and Omar Issing, one of the key members of the bank's board, answered outright that they couldn't. The answer is somewhat incorrect since any country can unilaterally "eurorize" or "dollarize" and does not need the stamp of approval of the ECB. As a matter of fact, in many countries market participants make such a decision, which is to use a foreign currency as a substitute for their own currency irrespective of whether this is formally endorsed by their government. In Bulgaria, for example, more than 40 percent of all bank deposits are in foreign currency (mostly euros) rather than leva. Hence foreign currency in Bulgaria plays an important role as a store of value. The position by the ECB to "prohibit" accession countries from adopting the euro unilaterally is not based on economics, and the ECB should reevaluate its position. Indeed, Bulgaria could be a candidate for eurorization, especially if the accession discussions become protracted.

Another questionable issue that relates specifically to countries that have a currency board arrangement and that are fortunate enough to have large productivity gains in the tradable sector refers to the Maastricht criteria on inflation. According to the Maastricht criteria, a country that wants to adopt the euro cannot have an inflation rate that exceeds the average of the three lowest inflation rates in EMU countries. As Mr. Buiter and others have pointed out, because of the Samuelson-Belassa effect, such a rule does not make a lot of sense for countries with strong productivity growth. As a matter of fact, it could lead to non-market interventions through price ceilings and changes in the tax system in order to artificially lower the inflation rate. Rather than encouraging accession countries to engage in non-market behavior, the EU and ECB should revaluate their Maastricht criteria and take into account new realities.

Furthermore, on the way to EMU membership, accession countries are asked to be part of the Exchange Rate Mechanism 2 (ERM2) for two years. Such a requirement appears necessary for countries that used a somewhat flexible exchange rate system before. This period could then prepare market participants for the next step, that is, the most extreme version of a fixed exchange rate system, the adoption of the euro. The need for such a transition period is less clear if a country demonstrated over a prolonged period of time – in the case of Bulgaria an entire decade assuming EU membership in 2007 –that it can cope with shocks and react with adequate policy measures within the confines of a fixed exchange rate system. There is, however, hope for Bulgaria, in that if England were to vote in favor of joining EMU, the EU would make an exception and allow England to join without a two-year waiting period. Of course, whether England will indeed vote in favor of EMU membership is still highly questionable but after such a precedent, Bulgaria would have an easier time to ask for the same exception.

On a more technical note, Bulgaria and its banking system will be faced with the need to lower reserve requirements both to assure the competitiveness of its banking system within Europe and to comply with the 2 percent level across EMU countries. Given the adverse liquidity implications and the impact of the payments system, the ECB should provide clear guidelines to all accession countries that have a currency board arrangement for how to deal with such an issue.

Reference

Deutsche Bank Research. Key economic indicators: Bulgaria. Country infobase. http://www.dbresearch.de/servlet/reweb2.ReWEB?rwkey=u1562080&%24rwframe=0.

11 Bulgaria in a New Southeastern Europe

Robert L. Pfaltzgraff, Jr., Professor of
International Security Studies at the Fletcher
School, Tufts University, and President of
the Institute for Foreign Policy Analysis

Edited and updated paper based on the conference

By its history, culture, architecture, and political orientation, as well as its geography, Bulgaria is a part of Europe. Equally important, Bulgaria seeks to be integrated as fully as possible into the broader Euro-Atlantic setting. This includes both EU and NATO membership. Clearly, Bulgaria strives to become a full member of a Europe that is free, unified, and based on the institutions of democracy – a Europe that in this sense would be without precedent. Whether such a goal is attainable will depend on numerous factors that are now shaping Europe and the world outside Europe. They include the extent to which, as new members are added, a European identity will be more (or less) likely to evolve within the EU that produces a common foreign and security policy based on credible capabilities. Of major importance, of course, is the extent to which a unifying Europe would seek to work actively with, or balance against, the United States. This has been an enduring question for Europe and for the transatlantic relationship, highlighted again by divisiveness over the issue of international inspections and regime change in Iraq and by the efforts of France in particular to substitute a more multipolar global structure for the perceived "unipolar" dominance of the United States.

At the beginning of this first decade of the new millennium, the prospect for greater European unity seemed promising. Europe as a whole was preoccupied with further integration – the deepening and widening of the EU. At the same time Bulgaria, together with the other aspirant members, was developing its application to join NATO. Like the other prospective members, Bulgaria's success was registered in the invitation that was set forth at the November 2002 Prague Summit to begin accession talks based on a timetable in which NATO would acquire seven new members in 2004.[1] In the months following the Prague Summit, the deepening crisis over Iraq opened transatlantic fissures as well as tensions within Europe itself. Secretary of Defense Rumsfeld's reference to "Old Europe," juxtaposed to "New Europe," underscored the division between those governments that expressed sup-

---

1   Bulgaria formally became a member of NATO on April 2, 2004, along with Estonia, Latvia, Lithuania, Romania, Slovakia, and Slovenia.

port for military action, contrasted with those that opposed forceful efforts to assure Iraqi compliance with United Nations Security Council Resolution 1441 to dismantle its weapons of mass destruction. But it also provided evidence of other major differences within Europe – between the richer affluent Western Europe that arose from the ashes of World War II to achieve unprecedented prosperity and the poorer East that chafed under the heavy-handed domination of the Soviet Union for more than two generations and now seeks the fullest possible integration into the Euro-Atlantic community.

These divisions cannot fail to have profound implications for Europe and for the Euro-Atlantic institutions of the future. When three of NATO's European members – France, Germany, and Belgium – chose to block efforts to provide for the defense of another member, the utility of NATO as an effective alliance became questionable, and in its place the idea of "coalitions of the willing" composed of as many NATO members as feasible seemed an attractive alternative for the United States. As Secretary of Defense Rumsfeld has put it, "The mission determines the coalition." The Alliance that Bulgaria and other new members are joining will differ in ways that were not clearly foreseen when would-be members prepared their applications. It is likely that NATO members will participate in coalitions assembled for specific tasks or missions, although defense planning and training of military forces to operate together within the Atlantic Alliance will continue within the framework provided by NATO.

As recently as the summer of 2002, NATO appeared to be unified in its response to the terrorist attacks against the Pentagon and the World Trade Center. The Alliance had agreed immediately after September 11, 2001, to a U.S. request that contained several specific measures: stepped-up intelligence sharing; blanket air-flight clearances; enhanced security for U.S. facilities in Europe; access for the United States and other allies to ports and airfields located in NATO member states; and support for allies that might be attacked by terrorists if they cooperated with the United States (Gordon 2001, 93). Especially moving to Americans were the widely publicized reports that NATO early warning and control systems (AWACS) manned by NATO-European crews were being deployed to protect U.S. airspace to replace U.S. capabilities that were moved abroad to support U.S. military operations against terrorist forces in Afghanistan. Never had the Alliance or its founders foreseen that the Article 5 collective defense provision would be called upon to help protect the United States rather than NATO-Europe or that aircraft intended to provide early warning surveillance over Europe would be patrolling U.S. skies to help identify and forestall possible terrorist operations against targets in the United States.

After an initially strong and favorable European response in the form of invoking for the first time in its history the collective defense provision of the North Atlantic Treaty immediately following the September 11 attacks, the Atlantic Alliance in 2003 faced what was arguably the most severe crisis since its formation. In a matter of months the Alliance had been transformed, so it seemed, from an entity with a close-knit identity supporting the United States in its war against terrorism to a fractious, disintegrating group of states, some of which were actively seeking to undercut U.S. policy. An alliance based on the essential premise that a threat to one member is considered to be a threat to all, calling for a collective response, became instead an organization divided in its purpose and largely incapable of a collective response. This included debate about whether to engage in contingency planning as a basis for responding to an attack against one member (Turkey) sharing a border with Iraq. States that perceived no direct threat to themselves were not prepared to accept and act upon threat perceptions of allies. Even worse, in the case of France, they were prepared actively to oppose efforts by the United States to take action to protect itself against the weapons of mass destruction threat posed by Saddam Hussein.

Although the immediate crisis occasioned by French, German, and Belgian opposition to plans for the deployment of Alliance assets to Turkey was resolved, the issues that were raised cut to the core of the utility of NATO as an alliance for collective defense. However, NATO faced other issues of relevance as well. The United States had not made extensive use of NATO assets in the war against the Taliban in Afghanistan in the months after September 11. With a few notable exceptions the capabilities that other NATO members could have offered were not what the United States needed. With British support, the Taliban were defeated with a combination of precision-strike air power and special operations forces on the ground working closely with the local militias of the Northern Alliance. The Afghanistan war revealed again the growing capabilities gap between the United States and its NATO-European allies. The sums added to the United States defense budget in the months following September 11 exceeded the total spending of even the largest NATO-European defense budgets.[2]

To be sure, the Alliance had confronted numerous crises during the Cold War when the unifying threat posed by the Soviet Union had to be addressed. In the 1980s NATO-European governments had to cope with large-scale demonstrations against the deployment of intermediate-range nuclear forces (INF). A generation earlier France, under Charles de Gaulle, had withdrawn from NATO's integrated command structure and forced the relocation of NATO facilities, including its political and military headquarters, outside France. What distinguished 2003 from these

---

2   The Bush administration's budget for FY 2003 of $396.8 billion included an increase in defense spending of $46 billion. The increase alone amounts to more than the total FY 2002 defense budget of any of the NATO-European allies – the largest being that of the United Kingdom with $38.4 billion. The combined 2002 defense budget of the current eighteen non-U.S. members of NATO was $173.8billion.

earlier periods, however, was the unity of three core European members, France and Germany, together with Belgium, in their opposition to U.S. and other NATO-European efforts to plan for collective defense. Specifically the United States asked NATO-European allies to support a number of defensive measures based on Turkey's request for urgent consultations under Article 4 of the North Atlantic Treaty. The defensive measures included deployment of Patriot anti-missile batteries in southern Turkey, increased airborne radar surveillance over Turkey, and reinforcement of naval patrols in the Mediterranean. Even faced with strong domestic opposition, as in the case of INF deployment in the 1980s, previous German governments had supported the Alliance and the United States. For the first time since World War II, a German government placed itself in active opposition not only to the United States, but also to a majority of other European states. In the past, German governments had chosen to balance their interests in the relationship with Paris with the security requirement for a transatlantic link with the United States. Of course, an understanding of the German position requires noting that the Green anti-defense activists of the 1980s, including the present German foreign minister, Joschka Fischer, who were part of the demonstrations of that earlier period are now part of the German government.

The transatlantic crisis of early 2003 was symptomatic of growing differences between the United States and several of the allies, leading some commentators to question whether France and Germany even remained allies of the United States.[3] These differences appeared to be based on a profoundly different set of priorities and interests that shape thinking across the Atlantic about the response to proliferation and, specifically, the future of Iraq as well as the roles to be played by Europe and the United States in the world of the twenty-first century. Understandably, American thinking is filtered through the strategic lens provided by the war against terrorism and the suspected linkages between Osama bin Laden's terrorist network and Saddam Hussein's Iraq, with all that this implied not only for foreign policy and defense, but also for the broader transatlantic relationship. In Europe, the question of what to do about Iraq had led to a situation that could hardly have been foreseen by those who founded the Atlantic Alliance and the EU. The architects of post-World War II European integration saw the Franco-German relationship as its essential inner core. Without reconciliation between these two historic enemies, it would have been impossible to build a peaceful Europe out of the ashes and devastation of two world wars. It was assumed that around this nucleus would be formed a wider European unity that would provide a transatlantic partner with North America. Far from positioning themselves in opposition to the United States in what some U.S. pundits termed the "Axis of Weasels," France and Germany would be linked ever more

---

3   With respect to France, see, for example, Krauthammer (2003).

closely with their European neighbors and would act in harmony, if not always in agreement, with the United States.

Instead, the Europe that is emerging as we move into the middle years of the present decade is increasingly divided, with France and Germany, together with Belgium, having from the official U.S. perspective marginalized themselves as "Old Europe," to use Secretary Rumsfeld's term again. Far from providing leadership for a unified Europe, France and Germany have highlighted the divisions in Euro-Atlantic relations that exist even today within Europe. To judge from the Iraqi case, there is little basis for an EU foreign policy. Iraq has revealed a Europe that is divided between governments, not confined only to NATO's newer members, concerned about maintaining their transatlantic links with the United States, juxtaposed with France, whose goal clearly appears to be the weakening of the transatlantic relationship and the creation in its place of a European identity led by France capable of challenging and undermining U.S. influence and power, but not backed by effective military power. In what can only be regarded as an example of Gallic unilateralism, President Chirac warned would-be members that support for the U.S. position on Iraq could undermine their bid to join the EU. Chirac is reported to have declared that the behavior of Poland, Hungary, the Czech Republic, Latvia, Estonia, Lithuania, Slovenia, Slovakia, Romania, Bulgaria, Macedonia, Croatia, and Albania is "childish and dangerous" in not siding with France and Germany in the Iraqi crisis (Evans-Pritchard 2003). "They missed a good opportunity to keep silent… These countries are very rude and rather reckless of the danger of aligning themselves too quickly with the Americans. Their situation is very delicate. If they wanted to diminish their chances of joining the EU, they couldn't have chosen a better way." There can be little doubt that whatever previous misgivings the United States may have harbored about a common European security and foreign policy have only been strengthened by the transatlantic crisis over Iraq. A Europe dominated, or greatly influenced, by a French-German effort to undermine U.S. strategy and policy will be actively opposed in Washington, but also in parts of Europe itself. The United States will form other partnerships – whether multilateral or bilateral – with states in Europe and elsewhere if existing Euro-Atlantic institutions become obstacles to collective action rather than facilitators of cooperation.

The strategic logic, described subsequently in this chapter, that led the United States to support a major enlargement of NATO, has been vindicated since the Prague Summit. As the strategic frontier for Euro-Atlantic security moves to the southeast, the unwillingness of France and Germany to agree to support Turkey as a front-line member state casts serious doubt on the value of a NATO that would not have included countries such as Bulgaria and Romania as new members. As it planned operations against Saddam Hussein, the United States looked for support in the form of "coalitions of the willing" within and outside NATO. Facing opposition from three of the older Alliance members, the United States received expressions of support from the newest members and from those who aspire to join the Alliance. The military training, modernization, and other forms of cooperation that come with (and from) Alliance membership can also be available for use in coalitions. The Bush administration appears determined to take other steps as well to alter, as it is put in the Pentagon and elsewhere, "the U.S. military footprint" overseas. Specifically, this is likely to mean rethinking the numbers and types of U.S. forces deployed in Germany and South Korea. This includes the idea of forward stationing and rotating troops into different parts of Europe rather than the kind of permanent U.S. presence that has existed for more that fifty years. How new NATO members will be fitted into such planning will be on the Alliance agenda (see Curl 2003).

As a nonpermanent member of the United Nations Security Council until December 2003, Bulgaria subscribed to the "Vilnius 10" declaration of support to a coalition for the disarming of Iraq. Bulgaria's Council of Ministers granted the United States the use of a Black Sea air base and opened its skies to U.S. aircraft. Bulgaria also offered a nuclear, biological, and chemical (NBC) protection unit that was estimated to cost $500,000 per month, and the Defense Ministry increased its earmarked expenditures by a total of $17 million for the February-June 2003 period. Because Bulgaria's military airfields are not equipped according to NATO standards, the Council of Ministers decree allowed the use of civilian airports in Sofia, Varna, and Krumovo as reserve bases for U.S. aircraft.

Romania also offered various types of support to the United States in military operations against Iraq. On February 12, 2003, Romania's parliament voted to allow the deployment of 278 troops in a conflict with Iraq. Bucharest announced that it would assemble a unit specializing in NBC decontamination and de-mining, as well as military police and medical teams. The decision, which passed by a vote of 351 to 2 with 74 abstentions, reconfirms an earlier offer by Romania's Supreme Defense Council for overflight and basing rights to a U.S.-led coalition against Iraq. The parliament acted on a call by President Ion Iliescu, following Washington's request for support in a military intervention against Iraq. In addition to the NBC defense unit, Romania offered a military police platoon, a medical detachment, an engineering detachment, and staff officers to serve on the coalition's command unit. Minister of Defense Ioan Mircea Pascu stated that the Romanian offer would cost around $4 million per month. Bucharest hoped that a rapid victory of the United States. and its allies would allow Bucharest to recover some of the debt owed by Iraq to Romania from before 1989, worth $1.7 billion.

These offers of assistance on the part of countries such as Bulgaria and Romania are indicative of a broader emerging strategic setting that was the object of study by the Institute for Foreign Policy Analysis (IFPA). In a publication entitled *Defense Reform, Modernization, and Military Cooperation in Southeastern Europe*, completed in early 2002 and updated in 2004, the defense reform, restructuring, and modernization plans and programs of seven countries in Southeastern Europe were examined (Keridis and Perry 2004). In addition to Bulgaria, this study included Albania, Bosnia-Herzegovina, Croatia, the former Yugoslav Republic of Macedonia, Romania, and Slovenia. Each has been engaged in defense reform, restructuring, and modernization as part of its preparatory process for NATO membership. Each of the seven countries has unique starting points and challenges as well as differing political impetus and resource bases from which to proceed. As a result, the pace and scope of reform and modernization, as well as priority tasks, have varied among the seven. Learning from the preparatory experience of the Czech Republic, Hungary, and Poland, the aspirants were able to develop comprehensive action plans that will rapidly lead to NATO membership.

Completed with the support of the Kokkalis Foundation, the study was based on the fundamental premise that the integration of Southeastern Europe into the broader Euro-Atlantic setting is indispensable to the peaceful evolution, political development, and economic modernization of Southeastern Europe. In turn, the peaceful evolution, political development, and economic modernization of each of the states of the region depends on how their relations with each other evolve. In this process, institutions such as NATO and the EU, as well as the Organization for Security and Cooperation in Europe (OSCE), can play an indispensable role. As we saw in the discussion of preparations for NATO and EU membership, the standards for admission that are the established prerequisites for deciding who will be invited to join matter a great deal. Such requirements help shape the internal development of potential members in a whole host of ways – ensuring civilian control of the military and transparency of defense budgets, furnishing incentives for defense restructuring and modernization, and providing a basis as well as incentives for economic growth. How Bulgaria and the other aspirant NATO members are preparing themselves for such membership was the object of extensive analysis in the study, recognizing as it did the vital importance attached to their progressive integration into these international institutions.

As we think about Euro-Atlantic institutions in the early twenty-first century, it is instructive to consider the chronological relationship between political-military and economic institutions. The formation of the Atlantic Alliance in 1949 preceded by several years the European Economic Community, as the EU was known in those days. NATO underwent its first two enlargements with the admission of Greece and Turkey in 1952 and the Federal Republic of Germany in 1955. The expansion of NATO in the twenty-first century has preceded the admission of new members to the EU as it did in the late 1990s. It is appropriate that an institution providing for political-military security should be in place in advance or at least alongside of an organization such as the EU for economic integration. This assertion is based on recognition that political-military security is the essential prerequisite to long-term economic development. Ethno-religious wars and other armed conflicts hardly offer the setting in which economic growth can be realized, as the tragic history of Southeastern Europe, especially over the last decade, so vividly demonstrates. As we look back over the past half-century, we see that NATO provided the security umbrella under which Euro-Atlantic economies could flourish in the Cold War era. This relationship between security and economic growth continues in the twenty-first century, but only if there remains a set of common interests leading to agreement on collective action. Or, to put this in a more contemporary context, how we fight and win the war against terrorism will have profound implications for our economic growth and well-being. The cost of September 11 to the U.S. economy is still being tallied.

This leads to another set of observations, namely, the new geostrategic environment. For the United States, in the war against terrorism the question is whether enlarging NATO strengthens or weakens the ability of the Alliance to contribute to this mission. Do new members become producers of security or are they primarily consumers of security? The U.S. answer to this question seems to be that enlarging NATO strengthens the Alliance by giving greater strategic cohesiveness to a region of growing geostrategic importance. With Bulgaria and the other Southeastern European applicants as Alliance members, we will have extended the Alliance into the region that, since the end of the Cold War and especially since the terrorist attacks of September 11, has gained new geostrategic value as noted elsewhere in this chapter. Even before September 11, the geostrategic importance of the region that encompasses the littorals of the Black Sea and extends eastward into Central and South Asia was widely recognized. The region between the Black Sea and the Caspian forms an important point of geostrategic intersection of great or aspirant powers based on energy sources and pipelines. It is also an arena of ethno-religious conflict and a base for terrorist operations. Bulgaria, along with Romania, is pivotal to the broader region that includes countries surrounding the Black Sea and also encompasses Southeastern Europe and extends into Central Asia. Along with Romania, Bulgaria's accession will provide land and other links with current NATO members such as Greece, Turkey, and Hungary. The possibility of NATO access to military facilities in Bulgaria and the ongoing and planned modernization and restructuring of defense forces enhance Bulgaria's attractiveness as a NATO member.

The ability of Bulgaria to conduct NATO-standard peace operations, based on integrated training, equipment, and command structure, will be important if Bulgaria and other potential new members are to be producers of security. Stated differently, the proponents of NATO enlargement seek to reconcile inclusiveness with effectiveness, measured both in political and military terms. Here it is important to underscore Bulgaria's support not only during operation Allied Force in 1999, but also its more recent agreement to allow overflight, transit, and access to Bulgarian territory for military personnel and equipment from the United States and other coalition partners as a staging area for operation Enduring Freedom in Afghanistan. As already noted, Bulgaria has been asked again to provide logistical support as other targets in the war against terrorism are identified and struck. In fact, Bulgaria has made contributions such as it would have been expected to make as a NATO member. This statement is not meant to take Bulgaria for granted, but instead to reinforce the point that Bulgaria fits fully into the emerging geostrategic map that is taking shape as we wage the war against terrorism. Obviously, much more needs to be done to realize the potential for effective use of NATO in this effort. This includes greater efforts in the sharing of intelligence information and equipping defense forces of new and prospective (as well as existing) NATO members for the spectrum of operations in the new, post-September 11 security paradigm. Further, it includes efforts to continue to modernize and integrate air traffic control operations with upgrades to Bulgaria's air sovereignty operations center. Both Bulgaria and Romania could be considered as missile defense deployment sites depending on the architecture that is developed for missile defense. Bulgaria and Romania may also lie in the trajectory path of missiles fired against targets elsewhere in Europe.

In the IFPA study on Southeastern Europe, several other priorities and challenges were discussed. Essentially, they include the development of strategies and capabilities based on threats to internal security and regional instability created by low-intensity conflicts, as well as organized crime (transnational and cross-border), smuggling (of drugs, arms, and human beings), illegal trade (mostly in arms in violation of UN embargoes), and terrorism that could threaten not only Bulgaria's security but also broader regional and international security. The existence of the so-called Balkan Route, the transport network for heroin trafficking from Southwest Asia to Western Europe, of which Bulgaria is a part, demonstrates an obvious need to defend Bulgarian territorial integrity and to cut off such illegal activities. According to Interpol and Europol reports, the Balkan Route is maintained today by transnational organized crime groups, all of which retain links along the route to local political, economic, human, and, in some cases, military resources. The events of September 11 only underscore the importance of cutting off this route and achieving this goal by means of more effective border and internal security forces.

Perhaps the most important challenge for new NATO members will be to adapt to an Alliance that is undergoing vast and rapid change itself, especially in response to the events of September 11 and the war in Iraq. Although NATO has been reinventing itself throughout its more than fifty-year history, as noted earlier in this chapter, the war against terrorism has dramatically transformed NATO priorities and shaped discussions within the Alliance. The Alliance that the new members have joined is in the midst of its own rapid change, as the Prague Summit and subsequent events related to Iraq have revealed. The Prague Summit produced agreement to create a NATO Response Force that would consist of rapidly deployable, flexible, interoperable, and sustainable land, sea, and air elements. This force is envisaged as having two brigades, or about twenty thousand personnel. It would be equipped with the most advanced capabilities and able to operate in WMD environments and other high-intensity combat situations. Such a force would reach full operational capability by October 2006.

How such a force would be related to the proposed EU rapid reaction force remains uncertain. The idea for the EU force was agreed upon at the December 1999 Helsinki Summit. It was to provide a European capability available for quick deployment in a crisis situation. Consisting of sixty thousand personnel, the force was to be deployable within sixty days with the means to remain in the field for as long as one year. The EU force was scheduled initially to be available in 2003. The target date has been pushed back to 2005, when the first of the battle groups will be operational, with eight more expected by 2007 (BBC News 2004). Even under the new schedule, the issue remains as to when the EU rapid reaction force could be deployable and how it would be related to the NATO Rapid Reaction Force. Here the principal difference lies in the role that the United States could play. The value of the NATO force would be enhanced by U.S. contributions in the form of equipment such as transport and intelligence assets. Nevertheless, the utility of such a force, like the idea of an EU military capability, lies in the extent to which there is consensus about its use. If such agreement cannot be assured, the value of such a force is dubious. Instead, as in the months after September 11, the United States is likely to seek contributions from individual Alliance members, or from prospective members, in its military operations against terrorism.

Agreement was also reached at the Prague Summit to streamline NATO's military command arrangements. These would be designed to provide a leaner command structure consisting of two strategic commands. The two commands would include the strategic command for operations with headquarters in Belgium, supported by two Joint Force commands able to generate a land-based Combined Joint Task Force (CJTF) headquarters and a standing joint headquarters from which a sea-based CJTF could be developed. The new structure would also include a strategic command for transformation, with headquarters in the United States and a presence in Europe. This command would have among its responsibilities the task of promoting the modernization and interoperability of forces committed to the Alliance.

Specifically, NATO will need to develop capabilities based on planning, exercises, and training for military operations and consequence management. It has already been agreed that such initiatives and capabilities, in addition to the rapid reaction force, include numerous efforts, many of which fall within the overall framework of homeland security. This is an arena in which there are extensive preparations underway at each level – federal, state, and local – in the United States (see U. S. Office of Homeland Security 2002). Although there have been efforts to discuss necessary activities at the Alliance level, much remains to be done both to share experiences and insights and to develop and make available expertise and capabilities. Several specific efforts already underway, and discussed within NATO and specifically agreed upon at the Prague Summit, include:

- A civil emergency planning action plan for the improvement of civil preparedness against possible attacks against the civilian population with biological, chemical, or radiological agents. The Alliance agreed to help national authorities cope with the consequences of terrorist attacks, including those carried out with weapons of mass destruction.
- A prototype deployable nuclear-biological-chemical analytical laboratory that could be available when multinational forces are deployed, as well as a NATO biological and chemical defense stockpile, a disease surveillance system, and a prototype NBC rapid-reaction event response team. The NATO biological and chemical defense stockpile could require countries to earmark portions of their own national stockpiles specifically for Allied use.
- Efforts by the Alliance to strengthen capabilities to defend against cyber attacks.
- A "virtual center of excellence" for NBC defense consisting of linked (via the internet or otherwise) NBC centers and experts in the NATO member countries.
- A rapid-response disease surveillance team to cope with biological weapons threats, on which little has yet been done compared with nuclear and chemical response capabilities.
- A new NATO missile defense feasibility study to examine options for defense against the full range of missile threats and building on ongoing efforts within the Alliance to set forth alternative missile defense architectures.

Such initiatives, already adopted by NATO, together with other efforts, build capabilities to counter a range of asymmetric threats and will be the object of continuing attention. How aspirant NATO members fit into this evolving strategy will shape their own security priorities as well as their attractiveness and importance as

NATO members in this rapidly changing geostrategic landscape. The Prague Summit communiqué ended with the declaration that "European and North American Allies, already united by history and common values, will remain a community determined and able to defend our territory, populations, and forces against all threats and challenges" (NATO 2002). Events since the Prague Summit have posed new challenges for the alliance and its existing members as well as new opportunities for those who have been invited to become members. How the transatlantic relationship will evolve will depend on the extent to which the United States and Europe view each other as partners or rivals.

For the United States the good news is that the eagerness of would-be NATO members to join the Alliance is related to the importance that they attach to a link with the United States. For NATO's newer members, however, it will be essential also to strengthen their relationships within Europe. It is to be hoped that a more unified Europe will not pose a threat to the transatlantic relationship. Unfortunately, there is no clear-cut or major solution that will ensure that Europe becomes a partner rather than a rival to the United States. Contending forces will be operative in which the challenge for Bulgaria and its neighbors will be to reconcile their interests within Europe and in the transatlantic relationship. How those interests are formulated and harmonized will have important implications for twenty-first-century institutions and relationships within and outside Europe. What should be obvious on both sides of the Atlantic is the extent to which the Euro-Atlantic area constitutes a region of stability in a world of crisis and turmoil. That our ability to combat threats emanating from other regions will be strengthened by partnership and threatened by rivalry should be self-evident. That "Old Europe" and "New Europe" can be brought into transatlantic harmony with the United States is doubtful, especially if the goal of "Old Europe," led by France, is to diminish the position of the United States. Such a tactic appears both shortsighted and counterproductive. Its immediate effect has been to divide Europe. Its longer-term consequence could be to weaken necessary collective efforts to wage war against terrorism in a setting in which Europe, no less than the United States, is likely to be a terrorist target.

References

BBC News. 2004. EU approves rapid reaction force. November 23. http://news.bbc.co.uk/1/hi/world/europe/4034133.stm.

Curl, Joseph. 2003. U.S. eyes cuts at military bases in Germany, South Korea. *Washington Times* (national weekly edition), February 17-23, 18.

Evans-Pritchard, Ambrose. 2003. Fury as Chirac threatens new EU states. *Daily Telegraph* (London), February 18.

Gordon, Philip H. 2001. NATO after 11 September. *Survival* 43, no. 4 (winter).

Keridis, Dimitris, and Charles M. Perry, eds. 2004. *Defense reform, modernization, and military cooperation in Southeastern Europe*. IFPA-Kokkalis Series on Southeast European Policy. Cambridge, Mass: IFPA.

Krauthammer, Charles. 2003. The French challenge. *Washington Post,* February 21.

NATO. 2002. Prague summit declaration. November 21. http://www.nato.int/docu/pr/2002/p02-127e.htm.

U. S. Office of Homeland Security. 2002. *National strategy for homeland security*. Washington, D.C. (July 2).

12 Bulgaria's New Geopolitics

By Lyubomir Ivanov, Deputy Minister of Foreign Affairs, Republic of Bulgaria

Edited transcript of Deputy Minister Ivanov's presentation at the conference

The title of this publication and of the conference on which it is based, *Bulgaria in Europe*, is praiseworthy and deserves a few upfront remarks. Bulgaria is undoubtedly part of the European civilization community and will soon become a full member of key European institutions, including the European Union and NATO, the two most powerful integration mechanisms.[1] Bulgaria has placed a substantial amount of hope on the outcome of the NATO summit and the Copenhagen summit. As overriding statements made at this conference suggest, Bulgaria is a part of a new Southeastern Europe.

Since the end of the Cold War, Southeastern Europe has been identified as a source of new security risks. Paradoxically, the disastrous conflicts in the western Balkans also attest to the success of regional cooperation in Southeastern Europe. During the Kosovo crisis for example, Bulgaria became actively involved in efforts to build a consensus among the countries of the region and to find a political solution to the problem. Balkan leaders are, albeit with some difficulty, coming to grips with the fact that today's world is "globalized" and that traditional, political boundaries are no longer viable or sustainable. The proliferation of regional cooperation and regional organizations is an undeniable reality in Southeastern Europe. More importantly, in Southeastern Europe, much like elsewhere on the European continent, a new spirit of intergovernmental relations has emerged. What brings the individual countries of Europe together is a strong common interest in the future of European and Euro-Atlantic cooperation. A successful case in point is the estab-

---

1 At the November 2002 Prague Summit, Bulgaria was invited to commence accession talks with NATO. Bulgaria officially joined NATO in March 2004. As of January 2005, Bulgaria is a candidate country for EU membership. It completed accession negotiations in 2004 and is expected to join the EU in 2007.

lishment of C-BRIG, a multinational peacekeeping force that has its headquarters in Plovdiv, Bulgaria. In the spirit of the Partnership for Peace, the existence of this peacekeeping brigade stands as potent evidence that many of the negative stereotypes used to characterize the region are a thing of the past.

The 2+2 format, comprising Bulgaria, Turkey, Greece, and Romania, is another expression of the willingness and capacity of these four countries to contribute to peace, stability, and security in a pivotal area of the Euro-Atlantic zone. This cooperation is likely to continue in the post-Prague period as well, because regional collaboration represents an important element in the quest to consolidate NATO's southern flank and its interface with the Central European flank. Bulgaria's participation in such initiatives is based on an understanding of the fact that membership in the European Union and in NATO is chiefly a matter of shared responsibility. This shared responsibility will entail striking a balance between domestic policies, far-reaching reform, and the foreign policy line of integration. Above all, it is clear that Bulgaria's membership in these organizations will mean adherence to the system of European and Euro-Atlantic values. Bulgaria's accession to the EU and NATO is not an end in and of itself, but rather the most logical path to follow during the difficult period of transition.

In an era when globalization and mutual dependence are undeniable realities, security is not merely a matter of survival. Being in a key part of Europe, it is crucial that Bulgaria adopt a broader understanding of security that encompasses both development and prosperity. Southeastern Europe is increasingly becoming the frontline for defense against security risks. After the 9/11 events, Bulgaria acted as an effective ally of the United States in partnership with NATO. Bulgaria provided logistical support for operation Enduring Freedom and, for the first time, allowed an American air force base to be stationed on its territory. In addition to contributing to ISAF (NATO's International Security Assistance Force) in Afghanistan, Bulgaria has also tripled its contributions to SFOR and KFOR (NATO's stabilization forces in Bosnia-Herzegovina and Kosovo, respectively). Further measures to combat cross-border crime and to strengthen export control for dual products have been implemented. Not long ago, Bulgarian authorities succeeded in apprehending the largest known shipment of Asian heroine intended for Europe. In the spring of 2002 at Reykjavik, NATO reiterated its commitment to a peaceful, stable, and democratic Southeastern Europe, a gesture that Bulgaria partially interprets as a forward-looking admission of a crucial geostrategic reality: the security of Southeastern Europe would guarantee the security of the entire continent.

Bulgaria welcomed the extension of the SFOR mandates and the Bosnia-Herzegovina UN mission, contributing to both initiatives as a non-permanent member of the Security Council.[2] The international community's role, however, should gradually be transformed from one of crisis response to one of integration. Stability and prosperity in Southeastern Europe cannot be achieved with palliative crisis response measures alone. The best and most comprehensive solution to the host of problems facing Southeastern Europe is integration into European and Euro-Atlantic institutions. Given that Southeastern Europe is a region where ethnic and political tensions have the potential to thwart reform efforts and to lead to economic decline, following the path of integration is the only way to prevent the risk of isolation. For Bulgaria, the political objectives of lasting peace and respect for human rights are closely related to the objective of economic prosperity. Multilateral cooperation represents an important means for reforming Bulgaria's economic infrastructure and generating technological emancipation, goals that must be met in order to overcome the region's lag in modernization and to expand the zone of stability in Europe.

The European Union is already negotiating with Bulgaria and Romania for accession and it has started a stabilization and association process with the western Balkans. Active in Bosnia-Herzegovina, Kosovo, and the Republic of Macedonia, NATO has succeeded in overcoming the consequences associated with the collapse of the former Yugoslavia. At the Prague Summit, the EU and NATO took the chance to continue this success by inviting the best-prepared candidate countries to join their respective institutions. Already, NATO and the EU have given signals that countries that consistently score high in reform and are in a position to contribute to regional stability will be invited. At Barcelona, the delegates of the parliamentary Assembly of NATO were united on the issue of NATO enlargement. The final declaration focused on a massive and robust enlargement that would include, and was therefore naturally supported by, Bulgaria. Bulgaria was not complacent and the Prague meeting was the hallmark of a new phase in Bulgaria's relations with NATO.

More work must be done to counter corruption and organized crime and to increase the efficiency of judicial and military reform in Bulgaria. Although the enlargement decision is primarily political in nature, it should be emphasized that significant defense rationales exist to support Bulgaria's bid for full integration into the EU and NATO. Bulgaria has been working diligently to meet the defense requirements for membership, including those provisions implied in Article 5. These objectives will be part of the Fourth National Program within the framework of the Accession to NATO Plan, which had started already and has continued after Prague. The implementation of the above measures has been guaranteed by Bul-

---

2   The United Nations Mission in Bosnia and Herzegovina (UNMIBH) was set up in 1995, and it performed a number of functions related to law enforcement activities and police reform. The European Union Police Mission took over for UNMIBH on 1 January 2003. SFOR concluded its mission on 2 December 2004 and was replaced by EUFOR, an EU force of seven thousand..

garia's military budget, which as a proportion of GDP is the highest of any of the candidate countries.

In conclusion, I would like to emphasize that the European framework means shared values, but it also means the development of a common European infrastructure network. Today, Europe needs to accelerate the implementation of major infrastructure development projects. Massive investment in infrastructure development that will facilitate communication across borders is necessary along pan-European Corridors 4 and 8. Bulgaria needs normal links with the rest of Europe, which will help open new market prospects and will generally enhance economic cooperation. Furthermore, these links will increase the relative importance of the region both within European structures and internationally. Most importantly, infrastructure improvements will help speed the adoption of European standards and integration values in Bulgaria, effectively abolishing the real reasons for conflict, which are poverty and underdevelopment.

13 Economic Stabilization in Bulgaria and the Road toward Modernization

By Sofia Kassidova, Deputy Minister of the Economy, Republic of Bulgaria

Edited transcript of Deputy Minister Kassidova's presentation at the conference

The economic policy of the Bulgarian government is based on three major economic frameworks. The first of these frameworks is the agreement with the IMF for 2002 and 2003, which targets the macroeconomic and fiscal stability of the country. The second is Bulgaria's three-year agreement with the World Bank consisting of bold structural reform measures, which is discussed in more detail later. This agreement with the World Bank is also connected to a bad-case scenario funding of $700 million, $400 million of which will be for balance of payments support and the rest for investment projects. The third framework of Bulgarian structural reforms comes from the adoption of the *acquis*, the European Union legislation that provides for the establishment of institutions in this country and also for the application of EU law. As Ambassador Kourkoulas said, Bulgaria has made enormous progress in adopting the *acquis*, closing so far twenty chapters of these negotiations.[1] However, there is a need to further speed up this process and a need to finalize structural reforms in Bulgaria if the nation wants to have a fully functioning market economy.

So, in brief, what are the main pillars of Bulgaria's economic policy program? In the first place, Bulgaria must sustain the already implemented structural reforms by finalizing wide-scale privatization and completing the privatization of the remaining minority stakes in the state-owned enterprises. Later this year [2002], we plan to complete the sale of telecom operator BTC[2], Biochim Commercial Bank, and most probably others. As will be announced soon, the signing of the contract for Biochim Commerical Bank will take place on 26 July 2002.[3] This is an extremely successful deal with very good financial terms.

The second pillar, energy sector reform, is also in the realm of structural reforms. A new energy sector reform law is being drafted, and it may be implemented later

---

1 Bulgaria concluded its accession negotiations with the EU in June 2004.
2 In June 2004, a 65-percent stake in BTC (the Bulgarian Telecommunications Company) was transferred to Viva Ventures.
3 The contract for the sale of Biochim Commerical Bank to Bank Austria Creditantsalt was signed on July 26, 2002.

this year. Also, Bulgaria has a new energy sector strategy that gives priority to efficiency. Bulgaria has outlined a clear schedule for increasing retail prices and interests in retail prices, which was overtly made public. Either today or tomorrow [15 or 16 July 2002], the first very substantial steps in the privatization of the electricity distribution sector will be announced. The government already has selected an advisor for selling off the electricity distribution sector to seven electricity distribution companies.[4]

Another pillar of Bulgaria's structural policy is the strengthening of market institutions, measures whose main aim is to reduce market entry constraints and costs for businesses. Bulgaria is ready with a draft law on economic activity that has been prepared with the assistance of the World Bank and the Japanese government. This law will provide for monitoring mechanisms that will ensure that no regular regimes can place further limits to market entry. Also, some steps have been taken with regard to setting up companies in a timely manner. Bulgarian authorities hope that in three years [by 2005] it will be possible to set up a company in three days. Another structural policy measure relates to improvements in the delivery of public services at government offices. Some public service posts have been set up, but the government wants to implement more rigorous reform. For instance, before Bulgaria's agreement with the World Bank ends in 2005, the country would like to have a public office where public services actually can be delivered and paid for.

An additional measure with regard to strengthening market institutions involves ensuring the functioning and competition of the market economy. Enactment of the law on state aid may enter into force on 20 June 2003. This represents a very big step toward a competitive market economy because, for the first time, Bulgaria has established rules for providing permissible state aid to companies and for controlling, reporting, and monitoring this aid.

The fourth pillar of Bulgaria's structural policy is the deepening of financial markets and institutions. As mentioned earlier, first Bulgaria is going to finalize the privatization of the two remaining state-owned banks. Aside from these two banks, the only remaining state-owned bank is DSK Bank, which is the former state savings bank. Last Friday [12 July 2002] the Bank Consolidation Company announced a short list of five advisors to the government and DSK Bank. Once these advisors have been selected (perhaps by the beginning of September [2002]), Bulgaria expects to complete the privatization of DSK Bank early in the first quarter of 2003.[5]

We are beginning to see positive financial figures and statistics with regard to the deepening of financial intermediation. For example, credits extended to non-financial institutions have increased by 22 percent. Also, the Bulgarian banking

---

4   In 2004, Bulgaria sold 67-percent stakes in its seven electricity distribution companies.
5   The privatization of DSK Bank was completed in October 2003.

system is very well capitalized and provisioned. Non-performing loans as a percentage of the overall assets of the banking sector amount to about 3 percent to 5 percent, a very good figure indeed. Furthermore, some very important legislative amendments aimed at stimulating and deepening the banking sector have been made, giving the Bulgarian government reason to think that there is potential for big growth in this area, around 4.2 percent. The banks have very high liquidity preferences, so they maintain liquid positions abroad, but as the conditions and risks of business become lower, these assets may flow back into the economy and will then finance further growth.

The fifth pillar of the Bulgarian government's structural policy involves improving governance. Critical to this is the establishment of an efficient, unbiased administration. The Bulgarian government believes that one very important factor in providing an environment that is conducive to business is an efficient public administration. Another important measure is an improvement in the efficiency, effectiveness, and credibility of the judiciary system. Although there is currently a hot public debate on this topic, the Bulgarian government has a strategy for achieving this goal and has already seen some successes in this domain.

The last pillar of structural reform is investment and human capital. Bulgaria possesses knowledgeable human capital with great potential. With economic policies and particularly with tax policies, Bulgaria intends to tap the highly professional human potential of young people, who, it is believed, can work, set up businesses, and add value to the Bulgarian economy.

So, to summarize, the economic policy and, in particular, the structural policy of the Bulgarian government are based on the two following credos: Bulgaria needs less government in the economy, but growth, productivity, and efficiency should come up from the bottom (the micro companies, or SMEs). Furthermore, the Bulgarian government needs to provide a stable microeconomic and financial environment and an efficient and unbiased public administration, which will help businesses to function. With these credos as guides, Bulgaria can and will generate sustainable economic growth.

14 New Challenges for Bulgaria
by Kristian Vigenin, Secretary of Foreign Policy and
International Relations, Bulgarian Socialist Party

*Edited and updated transcript of Secretary
Vigenin's presentation at the conference*

The importance of any initiative that draws attention to the integration of Bulgaria into the EU and to the European perspective of the whole region of Southeastern Europe cannot be stressed enough. The conference "Bulgaria in Europe" was of particular value as it took place at a time when final decisions were being prepared for the twelve candidate countries (Bulgaria, Cyprus, the Czech Republic, Estonia, Hungary, Latvia, Lithuania, Malta, Poland, Romania, the Slovak Republic, and Slovenia).   In the months and years to come there will be a greater need for attention to the efforts, problems, and achievements of our country.

It is of great importance to realize that the European integration of Bulgaria is closely tied to the processes in the so-called western Balkans as well as to the smooth progress of the accession preparations in Romania. This means that Bulgaria is very much interested in a stable and developed Southeastern Europe with a clear European perspective. In this sense, in addition to the domestic efforts, our country has to develop an active regional policy, shaped around the common goal, declared by all Southeast European countries – accession to the EU.

We have to acknowledge that the use of the term "new" Southeastern Europe – as the second session of the conference has been entitled – is a bit precipitate but at the same time well grounded, given the positive tendencies in the region. Despite some setbacks it is obvious that the region has achieved significant results in its efforts to build long-lasting stability. The times of wars and chaos, religious and ethnic conflicts, totalitarian regimes, and economic sanctions are left behind. These achievements are largely due to the "growing up" of the peoples of Southeastern Europe, who have been able to define their priorities and opt decisively for the path of non-confrontation, cooperation, and democratic development. At the same time, one should not forget the crucial role that the international community and particularly the EU have played and continue to play in consolidating the successes and guaranteeing further development in the region. Several major tools embody the essence of the EU's strategy toward the region: the Community Assistance for Reconstruction, Development, and Stabilization (CARDS) program, the Stability Pact, and the Stabilization and Association Process.

Despite these undoubtedly positive developments new challenges appear on the agenda, challenges that hold considerable crisis potential. All foreign and domestic actors share the main goals in this respect, namely to avoid further fragmentation of the region; to ensure public order and efficiently combat organized crime and corruption; to increase the efficiency of the judicial system; and to improve public administration capacity. Of particular importance is the improvement of social and economic living standards and, last but not least, building up a strong civil society. However, one should not fall into the trap of generalizing the problems and prescribing one and the same cure for all countries. While the challenges mentioned are common to the whole region, including Bulgaria and Romania, there are factors particular to each individual country in the western Balkans. Thus, each country's path toward development and its reform successes will depend on how the EU tailors its general regional development strategy to the particularities of each country in the region. In this context, the situation in Bulgaria's neighboring countries like the Former Yugoslav Republic of Macedonia (FYROM), as well as Serbia and Montenegro, bear some examination, as do some basic positions to which Bulgaria must hold firm in relation to these countries.

The lasting stabilization of the Former Republic of Macedonia is of particular importance to Bulgaria for two main reasons: 1) its immediate geographic proximity to Bulgaria and 2) the emotional affinity of the Bulgarians to the Macedonian people. We have to support all efforts to overcome the crisis through the use of political instruments, and by supporting its sovereignty, its territorial integrity, and its internationally recognized borders, as well as by assisting in the implementation of the FYROM Stabilization and Association Agreement (SAA) with the EU. Looking back, we welcome the rapid response of the international community to the ethnic tensions and the armed conflict in the country, which threatened to turn into a civil war. The Macedonian authorities as well as the main political parties should be congratulated for the successful negotiation and implementation of the Ohrid Framework Agreement, which became a basis for the peaceful and democratic development of Macedonia. The general elections were a real test for the country, and the manner in which they were conducted surprised even the most optimistic observers. The transfer of power was achieved by democratic, fair, and free elections, a decisive step to ensure stability in the country. The fact that the new ruling coalition continues to follow the previous model of involvement of both Macedonian and Albanian parties in power is also an indication of a strong commitment to stability and peaceful coexistence and cooperation between the two main ethnic groups. The fact that the EU expressed readiness and later on took over responsibility for NATO operations in Macedonia was an additional guarantee for the peaceful development of the country while the Donation Conference for Macedonia, conducted in March 2002, ensured considerable support for financing reconstruction and furthering economic development. In addition, the CARDS program provided financial assistance in a number of areas: economic and social development; reform and training of police forces; customs administration; and the judiciary. It is important to note that, although the SAA has not yet entered into force because of delays in the ratification process in the EU member states, the Macedonian authorities are already strictly adhering to it.[1] The above factors, in combination with the relative stability in Kosovo, hold a realistic promise for Macedonia to overcome definitively the instability factors that hamper the country's development.

With regard to Serbia and Montenegro, it is in Bulgaria's interest to have a democratic, stable, and predictable neighbor. For years, relations between the two countries were shadowed by the irresponsible regime of Slobodan Milosevic. The wars and the related economic sanctions damaged not only the countries of former Yugoslavia but also the Bulgarian economy. The end of Milosevic's rule and the efforts of the present Yugoslav and Serbian authorities for reforms in all domains of social and economic life have changed the situation dramatically. The agreement reached between Serbia and Montenegro on reconstruction of the common state has consolidated stability from both a domestic point of view and a regional one. Of significance to the whole region is the full reintegration of the country within international structures and, as a precondition for this reintegration, full cooperation with the international tribunal in The Hague, which the Serbian and Montenegrin authorities have already offered unconditionally. The next step will be to sign a stabilization and association agreement with the EU. Such an agreement will open a real European perspective for Serbia and Montenegro.

The year 2002 saw a delay in the process of reforms as contradictions within the ruling coalition on important issues, such as those concerning Kosovo and Vojvodina, signaled instability inside and outside Serbia and Montenegro. The following year was marked by the shocking assassination of Prime Minister Zoran Djindjic. This fact attests to the priority that must be attached to fighting organized crime with immediate drastic measures, before it becomes a widespread physical threat to the political elites, to stability, and thus to the very basis of democratic political development in the region. At the same time, the way the authorities have dealt with this case, the support shown by the Serbian people, and the fact that this extraordinary situation did not lead to the destabilization of Serbia are positive signs of irreversible stability in the country. However, the democratic path of Serbia and

---

1   All of the then-fifteen members of the EU had ratified the SAA with Macedonia by early 2004.

Montenegro follows a stop-and-go pattern, with every step forward followed by a setback. At the end of 2003, the political landscape changed in a worrying way, when the Serbians gave unexpectedly high support to the nationalist parties. However, the democratic instinct of the Serbian people and, in particular, of the democratic political leaders will prevent the country from falling into a new vicious cycle of political tensions and uncertainty.

Positive tendencies can also be observed in the other countries of the western Balkans: the settling of the political situation in Albania, along with significant economic growth in the country; the drop in political and ethnic tension in Bosnia and Herzegovina, coupled with the normalization of state administration institutions and accession to the Council of Europe at the end of April 2002; and significant progress in the process of democratization and economic development of Croatia, a country that has already submitted its application to join the EU.

As mentioned above, the Stability Pact is one of the key elements to guarantee positive development in the region. The pact has created great expectations and hopes for significant EU support for regional development, support that would go beyond covering war damages and would focus on regional economic and social development. In practice, however, the enactment of approved projects has been significantly postponed and this delay has caused doubt and disillusionment. The prospects today are not any better – an EU enlargement of such an unprecedented scale requires tremendous resources and creates a real danger that the Stability Pact may be shelved, bereft of financing and political support. On the other hand, one cannot deny that with this initiative the EU has reunited the Balkans with Europe, and given a European perspective to the entire region.

At present, we can confidently say that the first stage is completed: the region is stabilized. However, any delay in the gradual shifting to the next stage – association with the EU – could undermine all achievements. Regional stabilization and EU association should not be understood as separate processes; rather they are to a great extent intertwined, as strengthening the association dimension will have a stabilizing effect. Moreover, the time to reconsider the current strategy is coming, along with the current EU enlargement. Clearly, the model of integration of Central and Eastern European countries cannot be copied and applied to the western Balkans without further thought because significant differences exist in the stage of development and in the initial conditions.

The process of integrating the western Balkans into the EU will take more time and more effort on both sides. But there are several simple steps that the EU could undertake: the implementation of enlargement instruments such as twinning, screening, and Technical Assistance Information Exchange Office (TAIEX) expertise; the use of pre-accession funds; and the opening of some EU programs. A clear signal would be either to put these countries under the responsibility of the Directorate for Enlargement or to create the position of commissioner on Southeastern European enlargement within the European Commission. The EU has already taken a huge step at its Thessaloniki Summit in June 2003, a step of great political significance, by giving a clear indication that the future of the western Balkans is within the European Union. This summit changed the situation not only for those countries but for Bulgaria as well. It is obvious that the process of building a united, stable, and prosperous Europe cannot be completed until this genuine part of Europe is integrated into the EU. Bulgaria's clear and confirmed prospects of becoming part of the EU strengthen its interest in pursuing economic and political reform.

As we analyze the priorities and challenges that Bulgaria faces, we must take into account the fundamentally changed situation of Central and Eastern Europe and the fact that the countries in the region have reached different stages within the framework of a common integration process. If we were to group the countries, we could divide them as follows:

- The group of countries that are joining the EU in May 2004, after successfully completing negotiations.[2]
- The group that includes Albania and the former Yugoslav republics (excluding Slovenia), which still face a relatively high potential for instability and are just starting the EU association process.

The attention today (and even more so in the coming months and years) is focused on these two groups. Attention is focused on the first group because these countries are going to live through the shock of accession and are in need of support – mostly financial – to be able to cope with the transition. Attention is focused on the second group of countries because in the case of these countries it is imperative that the process of stabilization be buttressed in order to guarantee that it is irreversible.

In this context, Bulgaria and Romania are in serious danger of being left in the vacuum between these two groups and out of the scope of international attention. Bulgaria needs to be exceptionally determined and to show clear resolve if it is to cope with this challenge and turn it to its advantage.

Solomon Passy, the Bulgarian minister of foreign affairs, stated in 2002 that if his predictions were to be proven correct, there would be ten weddings and two funerals that coming autumn of 2002. Building on the minister's humor, the worst-case scenario that Bulgaria could face could be as follows: NATO decides to limit its enlargement to five countries and postpones Bulgaria's and Romania's accession; the EU takes a political decision to grant accession to ten out of the twelve candidate countries, despite the fact that some of them are unprepared for such a decisive step. At the same time,

---

2   On 1 May 2004, the Accession Treaty entered into force, and ten new countries became members of the EU: Cyprus, the Czech Republic, Estonia, Hungary, Latvia, Lithuania, Malta, Poland, the Slovak Republic, and Slovenia.

the two left out have no guarantees or clarity on the terms of their future membership. The price of integration is so high that the European Union gasps for breath, focusing on this process and failing to pay the necessary attention to Bulgaria, Romania, and the other countries of Southeastern Europe. Meanwhile, in this scenario the United States gradually pulls out of the region. As a result, the instability in the western Balkans increases, to which the sporadic instability in Turkey also contributes. The old ethnic conflicts are revived and economic development slows down, which in turn intensifies social tensions. As a result of this whole complex of negative trends, Bulgaria falls into a deep political and economic crisis. The difficulties that the EU faces in integrating the ten countries and the new instability in Southeastern Europe cool any desire for further enlargement of the EU, and with this the prospect of Bulgaria's becoming a part of a highly developed community drifts away to a far-off future.

This worst-case scenario was not very probable. Further, the developments of 2003 proved that at least part of it did not come true. Since the theme of this conference was Bulgaria in Europe, an optimistic scenario deserves attention. Parts of this scenario have already become fact, with Bulgaria becoming a member of NATO in 2004 and already having a confirmed timetable on the way to joining the EU. Under the optimistic scenario, Bulgaria and Romania receive invitations to join NATO, which has a stabilizing effect on the whole region. Bulgaria is left out of the first wave of EU enlargement at the European Council's Copenhagen meeting in December 2002, but the country receives clear guarantees that the negotiations will conclude by the end of 2004, and the country will be able to join the EU on 1 January 2007. Along with this, the necessary financial resources are guaranteed, and with them Bulgaria at least maintains its current level of economic development, if not actually bridging the gap between itself and the new member countries. The integration of the new member countries proceeds without setbacks, removing all doubt regarding further enlargement, and Bulgaria becomes a part of the enlarged EU at an accelerated pace, based on the newly acquired experience on the part of EU and on its own roadmap. Along with this, the process of gradual association and integration of the remaining countries in Southeastern Europe into the EU proceeds, building on existing and enduring stabilization and growth.

No doubt all our efforts, be they at the presidential, governmental, parliamentary, party, or civil society levels, need to be directed toward the realization of this best-case scenario. There is still a lot to be done. Our society is not prepared for the challenges of EU membership, many people still do not understand what it is really about, and the huge EU approval rate is not necessarily connected to a high level of information regarding the positive and negative aspects of integration. Equally important is the issue of Bulgaria's strategy once in the EU, a strategy that has to give an answer to the question, "What would be the role of Bulgaria in the EU?" Further, Bulgaria must address the issue of its role in Southeastern Europe.

Bulgaria will do its best to help the other countries in the region to join the EU. The expertise it has gathered should be offered with the clear understanding that the quick inclusion of all countries, including Turkey, is in the best interests of all parties. With this it is important to emphasize the interdependence of the processes in the Balkans and in Europe. Today no country is capable of guaranteeing its own prosperity by confronting its neighbors. The only possible road is the road of cooperation, solidarity, and mutual respect, and all countries of Southeastern Europe now realize this. This is the road on which Bulgaria has embarked ever since the dawn of 1989. We hope that the time has come for Bulgaria to reap the fruits of its regional policy.

15 Bulgaria from a European Perspective

By Dimitris Kourkoulas, Head of Delegation,
Delegation of the European Commission in Bulgaria

*Edited and updated transcript of Mr. Kourkoulas's
presentation at the conference*

The forthcoming expansion of the EU represents a geopolitical move of the greatest importance.[1] When it becomes a reality, the European Union will have a population of almost 500 million and a GNP that by far exceeds that of the United States. The enlargement will result in a massive extension of the zone of security, stability, and economic prosperity in Europe, creating a better platform for confronting the region's transnational security problems. On a wider scale, enlargement will add enormously to Europe's collective voice while simultaneously giving rise to expectations that Europe will shoulder increased international security responsibilities. Thus, an expansion of the EU must be seen as part of a historic process that will shape the future political and economic geography of Europe.

The EU that Bulgaria will eventually join has come a long way from that envisaged by its founding fathers in the middle of the last century. There also have been significant transformations within the organization since work began on preparing Bulgaria for accession. When the Europe Agreement on trade with Bulgaria was initially signed in March 1993, the EU had only recently completed the Single European Market, and the Treaty on the European Union (the Maastricht treaty) was not yet in force. At this early stage, the EU – or more correctly at that time the European Community – exercised little authority in the realms of justice and home affairs, two areas that are now high on the EU agenda. And most importantly, the euro had not yet been introduced.

For the founders of the European Community, the idea of enlargement constituted a vision of a united, democratic, and prosperous Europe. Since its birth, however, the concept of enlargement has evolved into something more than a vision: it has become an irreversible and clear perspective that is likely to materialize within a relatively short period of time. The process of expansion has reached such a stage that it is no longer a question of *if* the prospective candidates will join but rather a

---

1   Cyprus, the Czech Republic, Estonia, Hungary, Latvia, Lithuania, Malta, Poland, the Slovak Republic, and Slovenia formally joined the EU on 1 May 2004.

question of *when* accession will occur. As the "when" depends on the preparedness of each of the candidate countries, the timetable for enlargement is largely in the hands of the EU's aspiring applicants.

At Copenhagen in 1993, policy makers agreed on the criteria that EU candidates are required to meet for membership. These objective criteria relate to the stability of legitimate democratic and legal institutions, the functioning of the economy, and the ability of the candidate country to assume and implement EU laws. In 1999 at Helsinki, the EU reached another important decision, of which Bulgaria was a direct beneficiary. The member states accepted the proposal of the European Commission to open accession talks with the remaining six candidate countries. Although these six nations, including Bulgaria, already met the Copenhagen political criteria, they had not yet been invited to the negotiating table. Looking back at Helsinki, one can say that the decision taken was undoubtedly the correct one. By agreeing to open accession talks, the EU demonstrated that it was serious about enlargement, providing strong encouragement and incentive for further reforms in the candidate countries.

Now to the issue of Bulgaria's preparations for accession. Overall, Bulgaria has made great strides to prepare for EU membership in the last few years. As is the case with all candidate countries, the European Commission follows closely the developments and reforms that take place in Bulgaria, judging progress on three groups of criteria set forth at Copenhagen.

The first criterion that candidate countries must meet before entry refers to the functioning of democratic principles. The idea of democracy is so central to the founding values of the European Union that membership negotiations will not even be considered unless a country adheres to this criterion. In short, the EU demands that countries possess stable institutions that guarantee democracy, respect for human rights, the rule of law, and the protection of minorities. Bulgaria already meets the basic political criteria, but further efforts are needed to eradicate discrimination, improve living conditions, facilitate access to education and health services, and decrease poverty and unemployment levels. As the above problems disproportionately affect the Roma population, attention to this minority group must be given priority.

The aim of the European Union, as stated in its founding treaties, is also to ensure economic and social progress. For people in the EU, this has led to a dramatic rise in the standard of living in recent years. The EU's dedication to economic growth and social progress is directly related to the second Copenhagen criterion: before joining the EU, a candidate country must enact the necessary preparations so that its economy can cope with the competitiveness of other member states. The economic requirements of EU membership present a major challenge and there are a number of issues to which Bulgaria should turn its attention. Firstly, the impressive macroeconomic stability achieved in recent years must be sustained and economic growth must be accelerated. This means continuing efforts to develop a climate conducive to business and investment. Laws and regulations must be put in place and these regulations must be applied in an effective and transparent way. Furthermore, to achieve such economic goals, the administrative system needs to be equipped with qualified staff and the necessary resources. Finally, the independence and professionalism of the judiciary must be guaranteed.

The EU is based on a common set of laws and regulations, known as the *acquis*. The third Copenhagen criterion relates to the adoption of the *acquis* and a given nation's capacity to implement it. Each member state has to adopt EU laws. As important and sometimes more difficult to achieve, however, is the ability of each member state to ensure that it can enforce these laws effectively and consistently. The EU is based on mutual confidence between member states, therefore mandating that any new member must achieve acceptable standards so as to gain the trust of others. The cultivation of mutual confidence is essential if the EU's cooperative initiatives, such as the internal market, are to work in everyone's interest. Negotiations with Bulgaria on the various parts of the *acquis* have been ongoing since February 2000. As of this writing, twenty-three of the thirty chapters were provisionally closed, signifying that Bulgaria has made commendable progress within a short period of time.[2]

It must be emphasized that the conditions for membership were not imposed as a means of delaying membership. Without the necessary preparation, enlargement will turn into a disaster both for the EU and for the candidate country. As the historical record shows, the conditionality exercised by the EU has generated remarkable success. The EU's approach has helped the countries of Central and Southeastern Europe to make the political, economic, and administrative reforms essential to modernization, which itself is a remarkable achievement even outside the context of EU membership. The home governments and the citizens of the candidate countries deserve credit for these difficult reforms, but the process was sustained through the support coming from Brussels.

Ongoing negotiations with candidate countries are an important and indispensable element of the European Union's work. Yet, for Bulgaria actually to join the EU and become an effective member, it is imperative that negotiations be accompanied by an autonomous effort to institute reforms in key areas such as the economy, the judicial system, and public administration. Nonetheless, the EU recognizes that preparing for membership represents a challenge for all candidates and demands much serious technical preparation. While the main reform efforts and preparation

---

2   In June 2004 Bulgaria and the EU concluded the country's accession negotiations with the closing of the final two chapters.

are Bulgaria's responsibility, it must be emphasized that the European Commission does its utmost to support this country in its efforts.

For instance, the EU has already provided Bulgaria with substantial financial support. In 2002 the annual Poland and Hungary Assistance for Economic Restructuring (PHARE) national program allocation for Bulgaria totaled over €122 million. In the context of the early closure of units 1-4 of the Kozloduy nuclear power plant, extra PHARE support was granted for restructuring the energy sector. The annual Instrument for Structural Policies for Pre-accession (ISPA) grant for environmental projects and transport infrastructure currently averages €108 million and the Special Assistance Program for Agricultural and Rural Development (SAPARD), a grant targeted at agriculture and rural development, stands at €54.6 million. Thus, total pre-accession assistance to Bulgaria now exceeds €300 million per year, more than 2 percent of the GDP.

How soon can Bulgaria join the EU? Over the last several years, Bulgaria has made impressive progress, giving the EU reason to believe that Bulgaria will be able to join the EU sometime in the near future. The accession of Bulgaria to the EU will be a historic event not only for this nation and its people but also for all of the Balkan countries. Coming myself from a Balkan country, I can easily appreciate the enormous, positive impact that Bulgarian accession will have on the entire region, an area often identified with instability, backwardness, and violence. If Bulgaria continues to follow the path of stability, prosperity, and cooperation, this negative image of the Balkan region will quickly become a perception of the past.

16 Bulgaria Ten Years Ahead

Petar Stoyanov, former President of the
Republic of Bulgaria and President of the Petar
Stoyanov Center for Political Dialogue

Edited and updated paper based on the conference

The Kokkalis Program for South-East and Central Europe at Harvard University's John F. Kennedy School of Government deserves honor and high praise for its wonderful initiative in publishing this book. Such a book about Bulgaria and its success on its road toward a democratic development is not only justified, but also a very timely deed. First, because after Bulgaria's forty-five years of Soviet history, the country had been living in isolation from the Western world. Bulgaria must be rediscovered by the citizens of the United States and Western Europe not only as a country of an exceptionally beautiful nature, remarkable history and culture, and a gifted people, but also as a country that has achieved astounding success in its post-communist transition through a lot of desire, work, and persistence (accompanied by inevitable hardship and sometimes even disillusionment). Second, the citizens of Bulgaria deserve a new and positive attitude toward the efforts they have made in this transition.

The Kokkalis Foundation defines its mission as promoting a peaceful, democratic, and prosperous Southeastern Europe. Let us not forget that the Balkan Peninsula – the other name for Southeastern Europe – obtained its name from the largest Bulgarian mountain, the Balkan. Regardless of the fact that politicians and analysts during and after the bloody clashes on the territory of the former Yugoslavia shyly avoided "Balkan" both as a noun and as an adjective, we Bulgarians keep taking pride in these notions, quite unjustifiably reduced to being synonymous with all that ends in blood and has unpredictable consequences.

That is why all that happened in the Balkans in the last decade deserves a much more profound, objective, and intellectual look. For instance, it is not quite understandable why the roots for the latest conflicts in the Balkans are sought in the two Balkan Wars (1912-13), and not in the time after those wars. Undoubtedly, those wars were cruel and fratricidal and ended tragically for Bulgaria. All European and American analysts justly described the horrors of those wars, and simultaneously noted with relief that such a picture could not be drawn in Western Europe. Unfortunately, this happened in Western Europe twice after the Balkan Wars – during the First and Second World Wars. Moreover, this happened in a much greater proportion, taking many more victims and displaying many more cruelties. This clearly contradicts the myth about the so-called Balkan mentality, which presupposes a bloody outcome for every dispute. For if this is so, what mentality can explain the bloody crimes against humanity during the Second World War, which sprang forth in the heart of Europe and produced the Holocaust, the ugliest crime of the twentieth century.

This is why it is naïve to look for a cause for the latest tension in the Balkans in a certain Balkan mentality. A much more reasonable explanation would state that after the Second World War, Western Europe defeated not only fascism, but, with the Yalta Agreement, communism as well. While Western Europe's peoples and politicians were laying the foundations of today's European Union, which condemns completely any philosophy supporting the forcible solution of disputes and conflicts, the countries in Eastern Europe, including the Balkans, remained hostages in a Bolshevik system that was based on violence. That prevented Eastern Europe from participating in the common European process of integration and from adopting Western standards of communication and conflict resolution. Thus, after its disintegration, Yugoslavia became easy prey for nationalism, which was as aggressively imposed by the former cadres of the communist nomenclatura as communism was imposed years earlier.

This exposé on Bulgaria's road traveled in the last fourteen years begins deliberately with these words about the "Balkan essence" of my country. Before the fall of the Soviet system, Bulgaria along with the other communist countries had been called an "Eastern European country;" it was thus discerned from its neighbors Greece and Turkey – both members of NATO, with Greece being also a member of the European Union. After the fall of the Berlin Wall, Poland, Hungary, the Czech Republic, and Slovakia preferred to be called "countries from Central Europe," bestowing not only a geographical meaning, but also a political connotation. Bulgaria turned from an Eastern European country into a Southeastern European country. If nothing else, the new label denoted in a better way the type of hardships the country was facing. On the one hand, the typical difficulties include building new democratic institutions and a functioning market economy, difficulties similar to those that the A-graders Poland, Hungary, and the Czech Republic faced and are still facing. On the other hand, more regionally based difficulties were caused by Milosevic's Yugoslavia, which turned into a territory of ethnic conflicts, and then into a territory of real war. Not a single other Eastern European country paid such a high price as a result of the Yugoslav crisis – closed borders, interrupted trade with Western Europe, the halting of ships along the Danube (a very important transportation artery), embargo, contraction of foreign investment due to fear of the conflict's expansion and to the overall instability in the region. All of these conditions created fertile soil for various types of smuggling along Bulgaria's western border.

In short, Bulgaria started its post-communist reforms in a very unfavorable environment. To attain results similar to those of the Czech Republic or Hungary for instance (especially in terms of the economy, where attracting foreign investment proved crucial for triggering economic reforms), Bulgaria had to make a double effort. The partial delay in reforms is not, of course, rooted only in the "Yugoslav factor;" such would be an unfair statement, but not taking this factor into account would be utterly unjust.

Since 1997, Bulgaria's society has paid a very tall price for the achievements the country has attained, and this is why Bulgarians have all the reasons to be proud of them. Moreover, up to the end of 1996, Bulgaria was in a very difficult economic and financial crisis that resulted from the rule of the unreformed former communist party.

When I took office as president of Bulgaria in January 1997, the country was in a really dramatic state because of the lack of political will to carry through genuine economic and financial reforms. The annual inflation rate in 1996 was 312 percent, in 1997 it was 548 percent, and the rate of GDP growth in 1997 was minus 6 percent. The energetic steps undertaken by the interim government that I appointed and the efforts of the subsequent right-of-center government that ran the country until July 2001 led to stabilization.

This trend was preserved also by the next cabinet, which is still running the country. These steps led to an inflation rate of 18.7 percent in 1998, 2.6 percent in 1999, 10.3 percent in 2000, 7.4 percent in 2001, 5.8 percent in 2002 and 2.3 percent in 2003. Real GDP growth in 1998 was 4.0 percent, 2.3 percent in 1999, 5.4 percent in 2000, 4.1 percent in 2001, 4.9 percent in 2002, and 4.3 percent in 2003.

Unemployment was reduced from 18.6 percent in 1997 to 13.67 in June 2003 and 11.0 percent by the third quarter of 2004. The credit rating has increased more than 10 times for the last several years, which is a certain indicator that credibility in financial terms has also increased.

After an unconditional privatization, by the end of the third quarter of 2004 the private sector accounted for nearly 70 percent of GDP. Interest rates are comparable with those in developed countries. The country's budget in recent years is balanced, while Bulgaria has restructured its priorities so that 60 percent of Bulgarian exports go to the European Union. The European Commission's 2002 Regular Report on Bulgaria's progress towards accession declared Bulgaria to be a functioning market economy.

Bulgaria's efforts to join the European Union and NATO are meeting with success. On 25 October 2002, the EU reaffirmed its support for Bulgaria's efforts to join in 2007. On 13 December 2002 in Copenhagen, the EU stipulated the date for the membership of Bulgaria – 2007. On 20 June 2003 in Thessaloniki, the European Union identified the date for the completion of the negotiations with Bulgaria – 2004. As of today, Bulgaria has closed twenty-five chapters in the negotiations with the European Union.[1]

---

1   In June 2004 Bulgaria and the EU concluded the country's accession negotiations with the closing of the final two chapters.

Bulgaria in Europe

On 22 November 2002 in Prague, Bulgaria received the invitation to join NATO and in April 2004 it was among seven new countries to join the Alliance. On 22 March 2003 in Brussels, the Council of NATO signed the accession protocols of Bulgaria and the other six invited countries. On 8 May 2003, the U.S. Senate ratified Bulgaria's protocols for accession to NATO. Bulgaria and the other six countries met the criteria to receive classified information and were given access to the corresponding authorities of the Alliance. Afterwards, six more NATO members ratified our membership contract.

However, a discussion that limits itself only to the successes of a reforming Bulgaria (these are not only remarkable in many ways, but also unquestionable) will start resembling the boring reports from the time of communism. That is why an outline of some of the problems and challenges that Bulgarian society is facing today is appropriate. Furthermore, failure to solve these problems could call into question everything that Bulgaria has accomplished so far.

It is worth mentioning that, in one way or another, Bulgaria's problems and challenges are the same as those faced by almost all post-communist states, regardless of the fact that in Bulgaria these also have certain specific origins – on the one hand, the events in former Yugoslavia, and on the other the national characteristics of the post-communist transition in Southeastern Europe.

The euphoria that came to Bulgaria with the fall of the Berlin Wall is unforgettable: one of the saddest symbols of European division collapsed without a single victim. Considering the two world wars and especially the Cold War, the uniqueness of this historical transition was astounding. The unexpectedness and the ease of this event brought with them the illusion that the transition to a united Europe would be as easy as the fall of the Wall. Fourteen years later, one sees clearly that the problems and the challenges of European integration are much more difficult than anyone imagined.

At the beginning, we thought that the establishment of democratic institutions after the collapse of the totalitarian state would be the greatest task facing the former socialist states. This, however, was accomplished relatively easily. The EU's and Council of Europe's reports declare that Bulgaria, like most of the former communist states of Eastern Europe, today has functioning democratic institutions and developing civil societies. Democratic elections are held everywhere, freedom of speech and press is a fact, freedom of association is also a fact, citizens are equal in terms of the law, and multiparty systems are everywhere. The completion of the political criteria is a fact for every EU-membership candidate.

This, of course, is not enough. Democracy in the post-communist societies will remain rather fragile unless institutional and legislative mechanisms, an efficient judiciary, state administration, and police, and a responsible civil society bolster it.

And this is where Bulgaria, and most of the post-communist states in Europe, is having the greatest of difficulties. Most public opinion polls in these countries show an increasing sense of insecurity among their citizens, insecurity about their jobs and economic future but also about their daily survival. It is true, of course, that under communism our citizens were deprived of basic human rights, such as the right of free opinion or to travel abroad. At the same time, however, the repressive regimes under which we lived would not allow petty or street crime to proliferate. Hooligans and offenders were persecuted with the same brutality as political opponents. In the process, the rights of a number of innocent citizens were violated but, then, human rights had no value whatsoever. As a result, one could see people walking peacefully in the middle of the night in major Eastern European cities, because the police were everywhere. This is not the case today, not in Sofia, not in Warsaw, not in Budapest.

This point is important because of its deeper and more dangerous implications. It is true that criminality is by no means an attribute of democracy. However, it is much simpler for a problem of the democratization process to be defined as a problem of democracy, thus raising doubts about the very nature of democratic government.

Incidentally, one of our delusions after the lifting of the Iron Curtain was that democratic government and a strong state are not directly interdependent. The totalitarian state, which controlled our entire life, had become so abhorrent to us that many perceived the state in general as a threat to the emerging Eastern European democracies. Happily, in Bulgaria we did not go so far as to throw the baby out with the bath water.

Today, it is more than obvious that democracy fully corresponds to the notion of a strong state that effectively looks after law and order and the peace and security of its citizens without violating their rights and freedoms. However, after having reached this conclusion both the Bulgarian citizens and Bulgarian politicians are now facing the very serious task of reforming the judicial system and providing conditions (not only legislative) for it to work in synchrony with the police, court authorities, and civil society. Today, this reform is the most important expectation of the Bulgarian citizenry, and most certainly a properly functioning judicial system is *the* sine qua non for the successful functioning of any democratic state.

Despite everything said so far, economic reforms and their consequences continue to be the most serious challenge for the countries in transition. This is clearly demonstrated in Bulgaria. This fact dispels another illusion born of the changes, the illusion that the most important democratic achievement for the citizens of Eastern Europe is the package of rights and freedoms they would gain after the end of communism. Indeed, this was the first breath of fresh air that the Eastern Europeans were eager to take. People wanted to form and join parties, different from the communist party, to travel freely abroad, to speak freely and criticize in public and, last but not least, to feel safe and self-important, rather than being just the nuts and bolts in a huge totalitarian machine.

During the last years, Bulgaria has achieved considerable progress in this respect. This was even stated in the European Commission's 2002 Regular Report on Bulgaria's progress towards accession, which gave a high rating for the success of the Bulgarian authorities in reinforcing and intensifying the stability of democratic institutions, reforming public administration, protecting minorities' rights, protecting freedom of speech and the press, and holding legitimate, free elections.

All politicians of the new wave who wanted to change our countries had focused our entire attention there, forgetting that the ordinary people felt attracted by the democracy of prosperity and not the democracy of poverty. So, in spite of the success with the democratic transformation mentioned above, and in spite of the obvious macroeconomic and financial success of the country, the standard of living of Bulgarian citizens is low. This fact emerges as a major problem, because the lack of a considerable increase in the standard of living not only yields disappointment, it also could destroy faith in the advantages of the democratic system as well as the meaning of the post-communist reforms.

There is something more important than the positive indicators, the GDP and inflation figures, when judging the success of a post-communist reform. This is the people's attitudes toward the changes, their determination to go firmly all the way to a mature democracy and a market economy without giving up halfway through, overcome by fatigue with the reform effort.

Bulgarians and other citizens of Eastern Europe regarded liberal democracy and the free market as the only attractive option during the communist regime. Today, the reforms leading to them are no longer met with the same enthusiasm. Moreover, they inevitably increase social inequality, which together with the corruption accompanying privatization is the worst "image buster" for democracy.

Eastern European societies are hypersensitive about corruption and social inequality, which justifies a discussion of the two phenomena and the link between them. The failure of the political elites in Eastern Europe to cope with these two problems could trigger doubts about the very sense and success of the post-communist reform of Europe.

Apart from its well-known negative impact on the individual, the public, and the state, corruption's most dangerous feature is that it erodes the very foundation on which the democratic institutions of a state in a post-communist transition are built. Public opinion polls show that it is not the poor or the losers in the reform process, but those who believe their country is corrupt, who are the most frequent champions of non-democratic options. Corruption and social inequality are the two main reasons why sentiments of what we call post-communist nostalgia have crept in among the public of former communist countries. This phenomenon makes some people even dream of the "firm hand" or "the strong man" who would punish the corrupt politicians, magistrates, and bureaucrats, allowing the citizens to breathe a sigh of relief. In other words, corruption and its disgusting metastases have prompted people for whom democracy used to be the only way out for their countries after the collapse of communism to dream of what is in fact the opposite of that same democracy. Corruption and social inequality do not simply break people's faith in the advantages of democratic government; they provoke cynicism with respect to democracy.

This is why the idea that corruption is the offspring of democracy (the typically nostalgic misconception is that there was no corruption under communism) could prove among the most dangerous enemies of new democracies. This idea is as misleading as the belief that corruption is to be taken for granted because it is everywhere, including in the most advanced democracies. It must be recalled here that in democracy the public learns of corruption cases much earlier, thanks to freedoms of speech and the press, and unlike in totalitarian societies where ordinary people's presumptions about the magnitude of corruption can hardly ever be confirmed or disproved. Therefore, it would be wrong to conclude that in a true democracy, unlike under undemocratic regimes, there is no corruption. The difference between the advanced democracies and the undemocratic countries lies in the fact that, in the former, politicians and civil societies fight corruption whereas, in the latter, political elites try to use it for their personal or party enrichment, or at least connive in it.

Corruption is directly linked to social inequality that resulted from reforms in our countries. The citizens of Bulgaria and Eastern Europe will never trust their institutions or reap the benefits of the anticorruption measures that are in place if their governments fail to address with equal determination corruption and the drastically intensified social inequality.

Social inequality is not an unknown phenomenon in developed countries. But it is much more painful in the young democracies that only twelve years ago were still communist regimes. In these countries the so-called equality among people was most frequently abused. It was equality, indeed, but equality in poverty and humiliation: people were poor but equally poor, they had no possibility for free enterprise but this applied across the board. That equality meant civil death for the young, the bright, the talented, and the enterprising, and this is what brought about the implosion of the communist economies. Yet, the drastic change of the social order in Eastern Europe today (let us recall that the neologism "the new rich" was coined after the change) more often than not fuels nostalgia for the "good old days," especially among some social groups, like pensioners for example, who find it most difficult to cope with the present situation. (Unfortunately, the representatives of the left both in Bulgaria and elsewhere turned the communist nostalgia and egalitarianism into a synonym of social care – all attempts to dress up various forms of fiscal populism as social policy are proof of it.)

Here are the reasons for linking corruption with social inequality when speaking of the threats facing the new democracies in Eastern Europe. In the popular perception, corruption is the only reliable explanation for why in several years some became rich, while others remained poor. Why in some parts of Eastern Europe are there so many unemployed? Why, after all, are those who have committed obvious crimes against their own state still at large?

Clearly, it would be naïve and wrong to blame all negative effects of the post-communist reform on corruption. The fact, however, is that corruption and social inequality make people skeptical about the achievements of democracy. According to World Bank estimates, the difference in incomes in Eastern Europe is comparable to that in Latin American countries. However, in Eastern Europe, both social inequality and the abandoning of policies promoting social justice, more than poverty, may prove the greatest problem of the second decade of our transition. The question is how to solve this problem.

Besides, social inequality is by no means a notion from the leftist political vocabulary, which many deliberately avoid. After all, the term "social market economy" was coined in Germany during the Christian Democratic Government of Konrad Adenauer – apart from everything else, this term means a market economy with clear-cut rules.

As already mentioned, there comes next a functioning judicial system as a very important element in a new democratic polity. The Eastern Europeans need functioning and efficient judicial systems, which will provide people not only with rights, but also with the opportunity to exercise those rights. However, the matter does not touch only upon creating good laws by the parliament. The spirit of law-abidingness is much more important: the citizens' belief that the state and their lives are governed exclusively by law.

Finally, a successful post-communist transition requires investment in education. The greatest asset of the Eastern European democracies today is its young people; free of the communist past's mentality, they are energetic, intelligent, and full of ideas. Investing in their education, including the lessons of democracy, is the most significant investment for the future.

In conclusion, these lines on Bulgaria's advancement have been written by one who not only was president of the country during a dramatic phase in its recent history, but who has also been a participant in the process of its democratization since the very first day of the democratic changes. I have lived along with my fellow Bulgarians through moments of unforgettable joy, but also through moments of difficulty, bitterness, and even disappointment. Democracy has freed us from the problems of communism, which humiliated human beings, but it also has shown us the many other problems that we have to solve today. That is why the success of the emerging Bulgarian democracy is so dear to me – because it has been accomplished through the efforts of Bulgarian citizens, institutions, and non-governmental associations. The good news is that these efforts have not been futile – Bulgaria's success is recognized by everyone. The "bad" news is that these efforts have to continue for another decade, and then for another decade, and then – forever. This is the answer to the question, "When is the reform to end?" Never! Because Bulgaria's aim is to become a prosperous country in a globalizing and constantly developing world. And for this to happen, we must always be competitive, open to innovations, and persistent. This means that we have to be in a state of constant reform – safeguarding achievements, multiplying success, and never ceasing in our quest for better and fairer solutions. It is such a future for our country that we must believe in, because the citizens of Bulgaria can achieve it and they entirely deserve it.

Biographies

The Authors

Elisabetta Falcetti joined the Office of the Chief Economist of the European Bank for Reconstruction and Development (EBRD) in 2000, where she is country economist for Bulgaria and Romania. A graduate in economics of Bocconi University in Milan, she obtained her Ph.D. from the same university in 1999 for her thesis, "Exchange Rate Policy and De bt Management." Her post-doctoral research examines the empirical determinants of financial sector fragility in emerging markets, for which she was granted the Young Economist 2001 Award by the European Economic Review Association. Her recent publications include "Public Debt Indexation and Denomination with an Independent Central Bank" (with A. Missale, in *European Economic Review* 46, no. 10); and "Defying the Odds? Initial Conditions, Reform and Growth in the first Decade of Transition" (with M. Raiser and P. Sanfey, in *Journal of Comparative Economics* 30, no. 2). Before joining the EBRD, she worked as a consultant at the International Monetary Fund in the Western Hemisphere Department.

Martin Hallet has worked as an economist on Bulgaria and on EU cohesion policies in the Directorate-General for Economic and Financial Affairs of the European Commission since 1995. From 1990 to 1995 he was research assistant for European economic policy at the University of Trier. He has published several papers on the regional effects of European integration.

Lyubomir Ivanov graduated from Moscow State University with a degree in international relations. He went on to study at the Institute for International Relations at The Hague, Netherlands, and at the NATO College in Rome, Italy. He has served as Bulgaria's deputy minister of foreign affairs since July of 2002.

Sofia Petrova Kassidova has been the deputy minister of economy since 2001. She graduated from the University of National and World Economy in Sofia and holds a master's degree in economics from both the State University of New York and the Central European University in Prague. Ms. Kassidova also received a master's degree in financial services and banks from Reading University, UK. She has written numerous publications on investment, privatization, and the development of the private sector in Bulgaria.

Laza Kekic is regional director, Central and Eastern Europe, at the Economist Intelligence Unit in London. Mr Kekic heads the EIU's largest regional team of analysts who provide economic, political, and business coverage for the twenty-seven countries of Eastern Europe. He also heads the EIU's Country Forecasting Services, which include the EIU's main traditional product, the Country Reports and the Country Forecasts (medium-term forecasts for sixty countries aimed at direct investors).

Dimitris Kourkoulas is a graduate in law from the University of Athens and completed his post-graduate studies in administrative and economic law at the University of Bonn and in economic law at the University of Cologne, Germany. He joined the European Commission in 1981 and was involved in the commercial aspects of the accession negotiations of Spain and Portugal and then in charge of the relations between the European Economic Community (EEC) and the Mediterranean countries. From 1985 to 1987 he served in the EU Department of the Greek Ministry of Foreign Affairs dealing with EU-Turkey and EU-Cyprus relations. From 1989 to 1993 he was a member of the office of Commissioner Mrs. Vasso Papandreou and was responsible for relations with the European Parliament, external relations of the EEC, development policy, and cooperation with third countries in the social field and equal opportunities for men and women. From 1994 to 1997 he was head of unit for political relations with Central and Eastern Europe. In 1997 he was appointed ambassador-head of the delegation of the European Commission to Lebanon. Since 2001 Dimitris Kourkoulas has served as ambassador-head of the delegation of the European Commission to Bulgaria.

Meglena Kuneva is Bulgaria's minister for European integration. She holds a PhD in ecological law from Sofia University and specialized at Georgetown University in Washington, D.C., and at the Oxford Centre, UK. She served as an MP in the thirty-ninth National Assembly and in August 2001 she became Bulgaria's chief negotiator with the EU. Meglena Kuneva was promoted to minister for European integration in May 2002.

Ilian Mihov is an associate professor of economics at the European Institute for Business Adminsistration (INSEAD) in Fontainebleau, France. He holds a PhD in macroeconomics from Princeton University. His research areas include monetary economics, fiscal policy, general macroeconomics, and the economics of transition.

Robert L. Pfaltzgraff, Jr., is president of the Institute for Foreign Policy Analysis (IFPA) and Shelby Cullom Davis Professor of International Security Studies at The Fletcher School, Tufts University. IFPA has offices in Cambridge, Massachusetts, and Washington, D.C., with a diverse program of studies, publications, conferences, and seminars on a wide range of issues. Dr. Pfaltzgraff has taught at the University of Pennsylvania, the College of Europe in Belgium, the Foreign Service Institute, and the National Defense College in Japan. He has also held an appointment as honorary professor at the University of St. Andrews, Scotland. He has been director of the International Security Studies Program of The Fletcher School. He has served as a consultant to the National Security Council, the Department of Defense, the Department of State, and the U.S. Information Agency. His professional interests include U.S. foreign and national security policy; alliance policies and strategies with an emphasis on Europe and the Asia-Pacific area; the interrelationships of political, economic, and defense policies; the implications of trends and projections of change in the emerging security environment; crisis management; and international relations theory. Dr. Pfaltzgraff writes and lectures widely in the United States and abroad. Dr. Pfaltzgraff's most recent publications include *Contending Theories of International Relations,* fifth ed. (co-author) (2001); *Strategy and International Politics* (co-editor) (2000); *The Role of Naval Forces in 21st Century Operations* (co-editor) (2000); and *NATO and Southeastern Europe: Security Issues for the Early 21st Century* (co-editor) (2000). Dr. Pfaltzgraff holds a Ph.D. in political science and a master's degree in international relations from the University of Pennsylvania and an M.B.A. in international business from the Wharton School, University of Pennsylvania.

Jeffrey D. Sachs is the director of the Earth Institute at Columbia University. In January 2002 Professor Sachs was appointed by UN Secretary General Kofi Annan as his special advisor on millennium development goals. He serves as an economic advisor to governments in Latin America, Eastern Europe, the former Soviet Union, Asia, and Africa. He is the author of more than one hundred scholarly articles and books. He received his B.A., M.A. and Ph.D. degrees from Harvard University and joined the Harvard faculty in 1980.

Alfred Schipke is a lecturer in public policy and teaches courses in international trade and finance. He has worked both in developing countries and transition economies and has provided policy advice to countries ranging from Croatia, Belarus, and Poland to Jamaica, Brazil, and Argentina. In his latest book, *Why Do Governments Divest? The Macroeconomics of Privatization* (2001), he demonstrates that governments are often inclined to privatize for politically motivated, short-term macroeconomic reasons that are potentially inconsistent with the objective of increasing economic efficiency and growth. Currently he focuses on public policy issues of "dollarization" and monetary unions as well as monetary and exchange rate issues related to EU accession countries, most recently with regard to Estonia. Dr. Schipke also works at the International Monetary Fund and shuttles frequently between Boston and Washington, D.C. He holds a PhD in economics and an MPA from the John F. Kennedy School of Government at Harvard University.

Krassen Stanchev is the executive director of the Institute for Market Economics and a former Member of Parliament in the Constitutional Assembly. As the initiator of the Balkan Network and the European Emerging Economies Network, Krassen Stanchev has rich experience in the region, and is one of the most quoted Bulgarian observers. In 1996 he received the best country analyst award for Bulgaria from *Euromoney* magazine. Dr. Stanchev holds an undergraduate and master's degree from St. Petersburg University in Russia and holds a Ph.D. in Philosophy.

Petar Stoyanov was the president of the Republic of Bulgaria from January 1997 until January 2002. In addition to having worked as a lawyer for fifteen years, Mr. Stoyanov has held numerous other posts, including member of the National Council for Coordination at the Union of Democratic Forces (UDF); chairman of the Council of Law with UDF; deputy minister of law; MP, deputy floor leader of the UDF parliamentary group; And deputy chairman of the parliamentary committee on youth, sports, and tourism. Petar Stoyanov has an MA in law from Sofia University.

Nikolay Vassilev was born in Varna, Bulgaria. In 1994 he graduated in economics from the University of Economics in Budapest and in 1995 he received a bachelor's degree in business administration, finance, and economics from the State University of New York. From 1996-97 Nikolay Vassilev specialized in taxation policy and finance at the Keio University in Tokyo, Japan. In 1997 he earned a master's degree in international economics and finance from Brandeis University in Massachusetts, USA. Mr. Vassilev has worked for some of the world's top financial firms. In 1994 he consulted the Investment Fund Varna, Bulgaria, on the legal aspects of instituting a privatization fund. From 1996-97 he was an officer for Japanese finance market strategies at the Analyses Department of SBC Warburg, Tokyo, and from 1997-2000 he was an associate manager for emerging markets in Europe and world emerging markets strategies at UBS Warburg, London. Nikolay Vassilev became the senior vice president and director for Central and Eastern Europe studies at Lazard Capital Markets, London, in 2000. He is fluent in Russian, Hungarian, and English and has working knowledge of German, French, and Japanese

Kristian Vigenin was born in Sofia, Bulgaria. He earned a master's degree in international relations and macroeconomics from the University for National and World Economy in Sofia, Bulgaria, in 1998. In addition to completing the KLN Executive Program on International Leadership and Economic Development, Kristian Vigenin has also completed a training program with the European Parliament, PES Group, Committee on Foreign Affairs, Human Rights, Common Security and Defence Policy in Brussels. Since 2002 he has been working toward his PhD at the University for National and World Economy in Sofia. Mr. Vigenin has also been working for the Bulgarian Socialist Party as the Supreme Council head of the Foreign Policy and International Relations Directorate since January 2002.

The Editors

Dimitris Keridis is the Constantine Karamanlis Associate Professor in Hellenic and Southeastern European Studies at the Fletcher School, Tufts University. He is also a tenured assistant professor of international politics at the Department of Balkan, Slavic, and Oriental Studies, University of Macedonia in Thessaloniki, Greece. Prior to his arrival at Fletcher, he was the director of the Kokkalis Foundation in Athens, Greece (2001-2005), and of the Kokkalis Program at the John F. Kennedy School of Government, Harvard University (1997-2001). He is a graduate of the Fletcher School (PhD. 1998, MALD 1994) and of the Law School of the Aristotelian University of Thessaloniki, Greece (JD, 1991). He has published extensively on issues of Balkan, European, and Middle Eastern security, nationalism, and ethnic conflict. He has been a member of policy planning committees at the Greek Ministry of Foreign Affairs and Education.

Charles M. Perry is vice president and director of studies at the Institute for Foreign Policy Analysis based in Cambridge, Massachusetts and Washington, D.C. He has written extensively on a variety of national and international security issues, especially with respect to NATO affairs and European security, defense trends and security policy in the Asia-Pacific region, non-proliferation policy, and regional conflict issues. Dr. Perry holds an M.A. in international affairs, an M.A. in law and diplomacy, and a Ph.D. in international politics from The Fletcher School at Tufts University. Recent publications include: *Defense Reform, Modernization, and Military Cooperation in Southeastern Europe* (2004); *Building Six-Party Capacity for a WMD-Free Korea* (2004); *The U.S.-Japan Alliance: Preparing for Korean Reconciliation and Beyond* (2003); and *Strategic Dynamics in the Nordic-Baltic Region: Implications for U.S. Policy* (2000).

Monica R. P. d'Assunção Carlos is deputy director for academic affairs at the Kokkalis Foundation. She is a PhD. candidate at the University of Athens and she received her MA degree in political science from Columbia University, New York, and her MS degree in management and policy from the State University of New York. She has also received a law degree (JD.) from the University of Lisbon, Portugal. Mrs. Carlos has participated in the European Union's Training and Mobility of Researchers program on the welfare state in collaboration with EKKE (the National Center for Social Research of Greece). She has published research papers and edited volumes on social policy, social democracy, and the welfare state. She has been awarded several scholarships and research fellowships by the Research and Technology Foundation of Portugal and by the European Commission.